Adam Spivey is the founder of, and head trainer at, Southend Dog Training based in Essex, England, which started back in 2012.

For the last twelve years, Adam has dedicated his life to helping dogs and their owners have better relationships. He always states that dogs are easy; the real challenge is the handlers and getting them to see things from a dog's perspective.

In 2019, Adam partnered with Evan Norfolk, his 'work wife', if you will. Together they launched an online training program that enables people anywhere in the world to get help with their dog.

Adam, Evan and Southend Dog Training take a no-nonsense approach to dog training, cutting through the jargon and simplifying it for the everyday dog owner.

Southend Dog Training, with a community of over 5 million followers, produces free daily dog-training videos across their social media channels that get straight to the point and are easy to follow. Adam feels blessed to be able to use the platform to educate the public on responsible dog ownership.

Adam is a father of three lovely daughters. He has owned many dogs along the way and trained tens of thousands of dogs, so he knows a thing or two about dog and child safety, and this is what inspired this book – one that is lacking from the market, but so important and close to his heart.

T0299648

Also by Adam Spivey

How to Raise the Perfect Dog

How to Train Your Dog

HOW TO RAISE
THE PERFECT
FAMILY DOG

Adam Spivey

A How To Book

ROBINSON

ROBINSON

First published in Great Britain in 2024
by Southend Dog Training Ltd

This edition published in 2024 by
Robinson

10 9 8 7 6 5 4 3 2 1

ISBN: 978-1-47214-949-7

Typeset in Sentinel by
SX Composing DTP, Rayleigh, Essex
Printed and bound in Great Britain by
Clays Ltd, Elcograf S.p.A

Papers used by Robinson are from
well-managed forests and other
responsible sources.

MIX
Paper | Supporting
responsible forestry
FSC
www.fsc.org   FSC® C104740

Robinson
An imprint of
Little, Brown Book Group
Carmelite House
50 Victoria Embankment
London EC4Y 0DZ
An Hachette UK Company

The authorised representative
in the EEA is
Hachette Ireland
8 Castlecourt Centre
Dublin 15, D15 YF6A, Ireland
(email: info@hbgi.ie)

www.hachette.co.uk

www.littlebrown.co.uk

How To Books are published
by Robinson, an imprint of
Little, Brown Book Group.
We welcome proposals from
authors who have first-hand
experience of their subjects.
Please set out the aims of your
book, its target market and its
suggested contents in an email
to howto@littlebrown.co.uk

I would like to dedicate this book to my children, two of whom are on the front cover of this book. They are the reasons I strive to be better and work my butt off, day in day out. I'm so proud to be able to have them be part of my journey.

I would also like to mention you guys: the readers – the ones who have taken the time to buy this book to get help for your dog – or those who follow Southend Dog Training and have been there from the beginning. It's you guys who make all this possible, it's you guys to whom I'm forever grateful, and you guys rock.

I know it's only meant to be one dedication, but this is my book and I can do what I like.

P.S. My team also need a thank you for making Southend Dog Training even bigger and for allowing us to help more people. In particular, thank you to my business partner, who came into my life a while back and helped build this empire.

Contents

Introduction

I'd like to start this book by saying thank you. It's something I don't think is said enough these days, but it's important to me. You see, it's you guys that have led to me to write not just one, but three, books. It's because of you guys sharing our content, engaging with it, booking our services for training or buying our products that I am here today writing this book. So whether this is the first book you're reading or whether you now have all three in the series; whether this is the first time we are educating you or whether you've been with us since the start, thank you.

This book is so important to me. It's dear to my heart and is something that I think all parents and parents-to-be who have a dog urgently need.

As a father of three girls – yes, that's right, three girls (two of them are on the front cover of this book, in fact!) – making sure they are safe around our dogs and vice versa is non-negotiable. Every day I get messages from expectant parents asking what they need to do in preparation for their new arrival, so this book is long overdue.

Did you know that in the UK, on average, three children a day are hospitalised by dogs? When you think there are more than 900 million dogs in the world, I shudder to think what the global figure is. And this number is on the rise thanks to a spike in viral social media videos, where people unknowingly put their dogs and children in stressful and dangerous situations, all for the sake of views.

Did you also know that there are approximately 250,000 dogs in rescue centres across the UK, and this number is increasing year on year. Most of these dogs are in rescue through no fault of their own. One of the main reasons dogs are rehomed is because of incidents involving children and/or because the owner didn't take the time to train their dog before introducing a baby into the family.

I understand how important it is to make sure a dog is well trained and understands the rules around them so that they remain safe. But it is equally important as your children grow up to make sure that they to know how to behave around a dog. In this book I am going to cover the dos and don'ts that are non-negotiable when it comes to children, dogs and general safety, as well as things your children can do as they get older so that they can be involved in the training too.

I will cover some common behaviour problems that you will see in dogs and how to overcome them. I'll also show you what you can do before the new baby arrives, because after all, having a baby is one of the most exciting and life-changing experiences you will ever go through, but it can be stressful in the beginning and your dog shouldn't add to it. You can avoid that added stress by making sure you train your dog before the baby arrives. It will make your life just a tad easier, and that's where I come in to help.

I think every family should have a dog. Maybe I'm biased, but there's nothing better than seeing a happy, healthy relationship between dogs and children. I couldn't imagine not having a dog (I currently have two). I have an eighteen-month-old terrier called Mila (she is on the front cover of this book). She is an absolute live wire of a rescue and I will be sharing some stories about her here. Then there's my thirteen-year-old terrier Roxy, who has been an absolute rock in our family and who we have had since before the birth of our children.

I want to share a story with you before we get stuck in, about something you absolutely need to know because it's so important: **never leave your dog and child unsupervised**. It sounds like common sense, but if you turn your back for even a few seconds, your child can get up to no good. I remember when Amelia was a toddler, we thought, *What trouble could she possibly get into left unsupervised for a second?* Well it turns out, all it took was a few seconds for her to climb into the kitchen sink. We found her just sitting there, splashing water everywhere. I still to this day don't know how she made her way up there like a ninja. It's one of those funny memories we look back on and laugh at, but also a stark reminder of how quickly children can get up to no good. Remember: dogs are easy, it's the children that are challenging! But all joking aside, you will hear me say it time and time again: for safety reasons, never leave your dog and child unsupervised – it's just not worth the risk.

One thing I know for certain is that this book will help you raise the perfect family dog.

CHAPTER 1

....

The best breeds for families

Although this book is largely based on you already owning a dog and preparing for your impending new human arrival, I figured it was worth talking about some breeds that I consider exceptional family dogs, just in case you don't yet have a dog. Don't forget, guys, our very first book, *How to Raise the Perfect Dog*, is the book you should read when looking for the right dog for you and your family.

NO.1 - GOLDEN RETRIEVER

Golden Retrievers are often considered one of the best family dogs due to their many happy-go-lucky traits. Here are some reasons why I consider the Golden Retriever to be well suited for a family environment.

Golden Retrievers are known for their friendly and sociable nature. They are generally very approachable and get along with just about everyone and everything, making them an excellent choice not just for individuals but for families too.

These dogs are highly intelligent, which makes them easier to train compared to many other breeds. Golden Retrievers are in fact the fourth most intelligent breed of dog (with the Border Collie in first place, followed by the Standard Poodle and the German Shepherd). They are very eager to please their handler and have the ability to quickly learn commands and tricks, which makes obedience training a bit of a breeze.

Golden Retrievers are known for their gentle disposition. They are patient, which is a crucial trait to have when interacting with children. They tend to be very careful and gentle around kids, helping parents feel more relaxed about the interactions between their children and the family dog. As I've already said, a child and dog should never be left unsupervised.

Golden Retrievers have medium-to-high energy levels; they are always ready for playtime and outdoor activities, and thrive on exercise and engagement, so are well suited to families with active lifestyles.

While they are usually not aggressive, Golden Retrievers are loyal to their families and can be protective in situations where they feel their family might be threatened. But they are certainly not what you would consider a fully-fledged guard dog.

They are highly adaptable to different living situations and family structures. Whether in a large house with a back garden or in a smaller, urban setting, Golden Retrievers tend to adjust well as long as they receive adequate exercise and attention.

They are very affectionate dogs that enjoy being close to their humans. This makes them wonderful companions and adds to the deep bonds they can form with their families.

Because of these traits, Golden Retrievers often excel in various roles that require interaction with humans, including as therapy dogs and in search-and-rescue operations. Their overall demeanour and compatibility with both children and adults make them top contenders for anyone looking to have them as a family pet.

NO.2 – BERNESE MOUNTAIN DOG

Much like Golden Retrievers, Bernese Mountain Dogs are also cherished as family pets, although they bring their own unique qualities to the table. Originating from the farmlands of Switzerland, these dogs are known for their strength, calmness and affability. Here are some of the reasons why Bernese Mountain Dogs are considered great for families.

Bernese Mountain Dogs are known for their gentle and friendly demeanour. They are particularly good with children, often showing a patient and protective attitude towards them. They are very affectionate and love to be part of family activities. Their desire for companionship means they bond deeply with family members, thriving in environments where they can be close to their loved ones.

These dogs are incredibly loyal to their families and are protective without being aggressive. This makes them excellent watchdogs, as they will typically bark to alert their owners of anything unusual but are unlikely to act aggressively without cause.

Bernese Mountain Dogs are smart and relatively easy to train. They respond well to positive reinforcement techniques, making them good candidates for obedience training and other dog sports. Originally bred as farm dogs, Bernese Mountain Dogs have a strong work ethic and enjoy having tasks to perform.

While they do best in homes with plenty of space to roam and explore, Bernese Mountain Dogs can adapt to various living situations as long as they get enough exercise and attention. They do particularly well in cooler climates due to their thick, double-layered coat.

They generally get along well with other pets and dogs if properly socialised from a young age. Their social nature makes them a great addition to households with other animals.

The Bernese Mountain Dog's large size (they are one of the giant breeds), coupled with their calm demeanour and deep devotion to their families, makes them especially beloved by those who can accommodate their physical and emotional needs. They are ideal for families looking for a big, loving dog that can participate actively in their lives and offer companionship and protection.

NO.3 - ENGLISH BULLDOG

The English Bulldog, with its distinctive, lovable appearance and demeanour, is also celebrated as a great family dog for several compelling reasons. Despite their somewhat formidable appearance, they are known for being gentle and affectionate dogs. Here are some key traits that make English Bulldogs great for families.

English Bulldogs are known for their calm, dependable nature. They typically have a friendly and patient disposition, which makes them excellent companions for children.

Bulldogs form strong bonds with their families and are very loyal. They love human attention and affection, often enjoying nothing more than spending time with their owners, whether it's on a walk or just chilling at home.

Compared to many other breeds, English Bulldogs require relatively little exercise, making them suitable for less active households or those with limited space. A few short walks and some playtime are sufficient to keep them happy and healthy. You always know when a bulldog is around because if you can't hear it snoring, you will definitely smell the farts!

While not aggressive, bulldogs are naturally protective of their families. Their sturdy build and brave heart can make them surprisingly effective watchdogs, despite their generally placid nature.

Bulldogs generally get along well with other pets if they have been properly socialised. Their easy-going nature allows them to coexist peacefully with other dogs and sometimes even cats. But bear in mind, a bulldog is not a breed that will back down easily if challenged by another dog, and same-sex aggression can be common (see box on p. 12).

Bulldogs are quite adaptable to their environments. They can do well in small apartments all the way up to large homes with gardens. They are equally at home in the city or the countryside as long as

they can stay cool; their brach-
ycephalic (flat-faced) nature
makes them sensitive to heat.
Bulldogs and other flat-faced
breeds such as Boston Terriers
are more prone to heat stroke.

Bulldogs are generally very sociable dogs when it comes to people. They are usually happy and enthusiastic when strangers want to say hello to them. Although they typically don't have a tail, unlike, say, a Golden Retriever, you can often spot a happy English Bulldog by its vigorous booty shaking. It is important to train them to greet people politely because although they are not the largest dog, they have a very low centre of gravity and are typically quite heavy dogs, so can easily knock over a small child unintentionally with their sheer enthusiasm. We go into more detail about jumping up later on (see pp. 41–3).

As mentioned earlier, bulldogs are classed as brachycephalic, which means they have flat faces. Because of this, bulldogs can sometimes have difficulty breathing and can be quite an unhealthy breed with an average life expectancy of eight to ten years.

The English Bulldog is ideal for families seeking a dog with a laid-back personality, moderate maintenance and a lot of love and loyalty to give.

WHAT IS SAME-SEX AGGRESSION?

This is generally when two dogs clash and can take umbrage with one another simply because they are of the same sex, for example male on male. Typically, this is because one dog is attempting to assert its dominance over the other.

NO.4 – VIZSLA

Vizslas are loved for their loyalty, energy and affection, making them excellent family dogs for active households. Originating from Hungary, where they were bred to work as hunting dogs, Vizslas carry some distinctive traits that make them particularly suitable for family life.

Vizslas are known for being very affectionate with their families – they are often referred to as 'Velcro' dogs because they like to stick so close to their family members. They thrive on attention and companionship, making them excellent companions that like to be involved in all family activities. Because of this, it is important to teach Vizslas that it is okay to chill out by themselves for short periods of time, so that you do not create anxiety-based issues, such as separation anxiety (see p. 44).

With a background in hunting, Vizslas possess high energy levels and need regular, vigorous and mental exercise. This makes them a great match for active families that enjoy outdoor activities such as running, hiking, playing fetch or even going camping. It's a breed that can be included in virtually any family activity that you choose to involve them in.

Vizslas are very intelligent and eager to please, which makes them relatively easy to train. They excel in obedience, agility and other dog sports, making training both a useful and enjoyable activity for the dog and its owners. If you do not sufficiently channel their energy through play 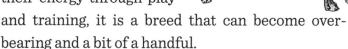 and training, it is a breed that can become overbearing and a bit of a handful.

They are typically great with children, especially when raised around kids from puppyhood. Their gentle nature and fondness for play make them patient and protective playmates for kids, but as always, never leave your dog and child unsupervised.

While Vizslas are friendly, they are also quite protective of their families. They can be good watchdogs, alerting to the presence of strangers or unusual noises with their bark, though they are not typically aggressive. Given they are known to be a vocal breed, ear plugs and wine are both recommended! Obviously I'm joking about the wine, however, the earplugs are required!

They generally get along well with other dogs and pets, especially if socialised from a young age. This makes them great additions to households with existing pets.

Vizslas have a short coat that is easy to care for and does not require extensive grooming – another benefit for busy families. Regular brushing, occasional baths and basic grooming routines are sufficient to keep them clean and healthy.

The two most common issues we see when dealing with Vizslas is separation anxiety (see p. 44) and resource guarding (see pp. 71–5). Vigorous exercise and teaching your vizsla to spend short periods of time by itself should alleviate separation anxiety. As for resource guarding, this typically stems from a dog that is bored and goes around stealing items, and then gets frustrated when you recover their loot from them. We see this more commonly in gundogs like vizslas and spaniels that were bred to hunt and retrieve stuff. Again, with proper vigorous exercise and training you can alleviate the chances of this happening. This is a dog that you want to work with, and that wants to work with you; this isn't a dog that is just happy to lounge around all day doing nothing, like the English Bulldog.

Overall, Vizslas are a joyous addition to any active and loving family, capable of forming deep bonds and participating in your family lifestyle.

NO.5 - MUTTS

Depending where and in which era you grew up, you might know these dogs as mutts, mixed-breeds, mongrels or even Heinz 57s. They often make some of the best family dogs, for so many reasons. Mutts are most commonly found in rescue centres, and many families, including my own, choose to adopt a dog from a rescue and give that dog a home. A common misconception about mutts or rescue dogs is that they are there because they are bad dogs. This simply isn't true. Most dogs in rescues are there through no fault of their own. Sometimes it's because the person who previously owned them didn't take the time to train them, so they just palm them off onto somebody else to pick up the pieces.

I have had three rescue dogs, two of which are mutts. There are many benefits to mutts. They generally get the best personality traits from the breeds of dog their parents come from and they tend to be healthier than pedigree dogs. They seem to get the best health traits from all the breeds they are made up of and a lot of the time will bypass the negative genes. Of course, like anything, there can be exceptions to the rule. My mutt Roxy has outlived my

Rottweiler and Staffie; at 13 years old she is still going strong. I don't know her exact breed, but she is a terrier mixed with something else. Mutts tend to have a very good life expectancy.

One of the things I love about mutts is the endless possibilities that are out there. Mutts come in pretty much every shape and size. You can get small 8kg mutts like my Roxy, or a 10kg mutt like Mila (the little dog on the front cover) to the 65kg mutt that I had at the training centre recently. They come with short fur, long fur, wiry fur, fluffy ears . . . you get the idea! And although you can get a DNA test to try to find out the glorious cocktail of breeds that make up your dog, some choose not to, like myself – I just find it more fun that way!

Many mutts possess great temperaments that make them excellent companions. Rescue centres can often provide potential adopters with detailed information about a mutt's personality and behaviour, helping match the right dog to the right family.

Mixed-breed dogs often inherit the intelligence and trainability of their parent breeds, which can make them responsive to obedience training and capable of learning various tasks and tricks. This makes them not only fun and engaging pets but also adaptable to a range of roles in their adoptive families.

Like all dogs, mutts form strong bonds with their families. They can be intensely loyal, protective and affectionate, providing companionship and love that enrich family life. Of course, there can be exceptions.

Often, adopting a mutt is less expensive than purchasing a pedigree dog. When you adopt a dog, you often have to pay an adoption fee, which is a hell of a lot cheaper than the fee you would pay to a breeder. Not only does that money go towards helping the rescue, but it helps cover the cost of any potential health treatments that the dog may have needed.

By choosing to adopt a mutt, families can support animal shelters and rescue organisations, helping to reduce the population of pets in rescues and contributing to animal welfare.

Overall, mutts make great loving, loyal pets. Their varied backgrounds can bring a delightful mix of characteristics, making each mutt a one-of-a-kind member of the family. Their adaptability and the sheer joy of discovering their unique blend of traits make them cherished companions in many households.

The reality is, ladies and gentlemen, these are just five dogs that make great family pets. In my first book I listed another five, which brings me to my point: any dog from a reputable breeder or rescue that is fit and healthy, that is raised correctly in a loving household where children and dogs are taught mutual respect, can make a great family dog. I added mutts as No.5 on my list because effectively that is what my dog Mila is, and she came from a rescue (she's my third rescue dog). There are so many gems in rescues. So let's now talk about a getting a puppy versus a rescue.

CHAPTER 2

....

Puppy or rescue (why so many dogs end up in rescue centres)

When choosing a dog for your family, you have to choose which route to go down. Should you go down the path of buying a puppy? Some people think of this as a blank canvas, as we get to raise the dog from the moment we take it home. Or do you go to a rescue centre and give a dog a home?

Now, let me be clear, there is no right or wrong answer here. It is ultimately down to personal preference and what suits your lifestyle. I have done both, and you might find, one day, you do both. I've had one dog from a puppy – that was Daisy, my Rottweiler. If you have read our first book you will know all about her mischievous ways, and the mistakes I made when I first got her. Since her, I've always gone down the rescue route.

I also had a Staffordshire Bull Terrier called Sammie. Sadly, she passed in 2022, but she was the dog that started my dog-training career. It is because of her that I discovered a passion for training. Given the fact that she was 16 months old and I had a two-year-old child when we adopted her, I wanted to make sure that she was trained and safe to be with my children. I also have Roxy, the 13-year-old mutt I mentioned earlier, and Mila an 18-month-old terrier mix.

There are pros and cons to both puppies and rescue dogs. Let's get into them.

BUYING A PUPPY

Getting a puppy allows you to do vigorous research on the breed that best suits your lifestyle. Knowing exactly what the breed is and their traits makes it much easier to have an educated guess of what sort of personality and tendencies the dog will have as it gets older.

Pros

If you get a puppy from a reputable breeder, you will know that the relevant health checks have been done, such as hip scores, elbow scores, etc. Hip scores are measured in nine parameters. The minimum score for each hip is 0 and the maximum is 53, giving a range for the total score of 0 to 106. Hip and elbow scoring is a procedure used to determine the degree of hip dysplasia in dogs and other animals and reporting the findings in a standard way. Typically, with a dog from a reputable breeder, you should know the history of the parents and their temperaments. You should also be able to meet the parents, which is a good indicator of how your dog may turn out. But don't forget, training also plays a massive part!

Of course, getting a puppy that you will usually bring home at eight weeks of age, you start with something of a blank canvas. It will be you that teaches many of the behaviours to the dog for the first time. It also means you are largely in control of its early learning experiences, such as socialising and exposure to all those things that your dog may encounter in its life.

Finally, there is something special about taking a baby dog (a puppy) and watching it grow into a bratty teenager through to an adult.

Cons

Do you enjoy your sleep? If so, read this very slowly and carefully. Puppies are much like new-born babies in that you will need to get up in the middle of the night to let them out to the toilet. They will whine and cry (but don't panic too much as it does get easier!) and they will test your patience.

Puppies, much like toddlers, get into everything, and you need eyes in the back of your head. Just like a toddler, anything that can go in its mouth will end up in its mouth, leaving behind those precious little chew marks.

Purchasing a puppy, especially from a reputable breeder, can be expensive. And we strongly advise that you do go to a reputable breeder. The average cost of a Golden Retriever from a breeder at the time of writing this book is in the region of £1,500–£2,500; sometimes it can be as high as £3,000. Conversely, the cost of adopting is usually around £250, so only 10 per cent of the cost. And although you may be able to find a cheap puppy on the internet from a backyard breeder, chances are you will end up forking out more in the long term to fix health and behavioural issues. We also need to make sure that we put an end to backyard breeding, and the only way to do this is to stop funding puppy farmers by not buying their puppies. If everyone did this, this unethical practice would eventually die out.

While breed characteristics can offer predictions, the exact size and temperament of a puppy as it grows into an adult dog can sometimes be uncertain.

ADOPTING A RESCUE DOG

Adopting a dog can be one of the most rewarding

things you do in life. This is why I have done it three times and don't plan on stopping. As mentioned previously on the subject of mutts, so many dogs end up in rescue through no fault of their own. It is nearly always because the owner did not research the breed, the breeder, or just couldn't be bothered to train the dog, and once it is bigger and more boisterous they decide they do not want it anymore. Another extremely common reason is because they are expecting a baby and did not take the time to train their dog, and now the dog is a problem. This is the exact problem we are hoping to avoid, and the whole reason for this book. There are, of course, pros and cons to adopting a dog. So what are they?

Pros

By adopting a dog, you are literally giving a dog a home that it would otherwise not have. You are giving this dog a second chance. And what could be better than that?

As mentioned in the list of cons about getting a puppy, they can be expensive. On the other hand, a very obvious pro of adopting a rescue is the cost, because it is a hell of a lot cheaper.

There are breed-specific rescues, as well as rescue centres that house many different breeds. In a lot of these rescue centres, you may even be able to find puppies. But if it is an older dog you are looking for, you will already know its size, coat and how it is going to look, etc.

Many dogs in rescue centres, particularly if you are going for an older dog, will likely be house trained and may have already received some basic training from the rescue centre staff themselves, which can give you a head start. Additionally, a decent rescue centre will offer backup support if you need it.

And did I mention . . . YOU ARE GIVING A DOG A HOME!

Now there are, of course, some drawbacks to getting a rescue dog, so below are some of the cons that you'll need to consider if a rescue is your cup of tea.

Cons

Some rescue dogs may have unknown histories and could have some past trauma, which can influence their behaviour and may require professional training. These dogs really are for more experienced dog owners.

Depending on the dog's background and previous care, there might be underlying health issues not immediately apparent at the time of adoption.

It's not always easy adopting a dog. Some rescues can have very strict policies on who is eligible to adopt their dogs. In some instances, if your children are too young, or they deem your garden is not secure enough or non-existent, you may not be a suitable match. Similarly, if you go to work for more than 4 hours a day, that could prevent you from adopting. That is not to say all rescues employ these policies, but I do understand them, especially the rules around children, because at the end of the day it is a big responsibility on the rescue. Still, it doesn't always make it easy for you.

Rescue dogs can sometimes take longer to adjust to a new home, requiring time to settle in and trust their new environment and family members.

One final con, although it might not necessarily be perceived as such to everyone, is that if you adopted a mixed-breed dog, the fact you might not know the full breeds can sometimes make training a little bit more challenging. We know that a retriever generally likes to retrieve (play fetch), we know that a collie likes to herd (or chase cars), but with a mixed-breed it's not always black and white. For me though, I actually find that a positive as it keeps me on my toes!

So in summary, there is no right or wrong answer. You have to do what you feel is best for you and your family. And there is nothing stopping you getting a rescue *and* a puppy further down the line. I do truly believe everybody should experience both at some point in their life, because, as you can see, there are positive and negatives to both. One thing is for certain, whether it is a rescue or a puppy, both will require training.

CHAPTER 3

....

Preparing for your new arrival and your dog's behaviour

One of the most important things you must do is make sure your dog is trained before the baby's arrival. The good news is, if you have only just found out you are expecting, you have nine months to work on these issues (and congratulations, by the way!). If you are just in the planning stages, then you will have even longer. As I stated earlier, a very common reason for dogs being rehomed is the lack of training they receive, and then along comes a new baby and suddenly that lack of training becomes problematic. I don't want this to happen here. So in this chapter I am going to cover everything from the basics that your dog should know through to the more challenging behaviours that may not necessarily seem like a problem now, but could definitely become one once your new arrival is here. An example of this could be your dog jumping up. You may absolutely love this and not yet foresee an issue, but when you are holding a baby and your dog jumps up, suddenly it may not be so cute. The goal of training your dog through the use of this book is to start training them as if the baby is already here. So let's start from the beginning with the basics.

TRAINING BASICS

If you have already read my book *How to Train Your Dog*, you will know all about the three-point formula that can help any dog, regardless of age and its behavioural issue. Follow the formula and their behaviour will start to improve tenfold. However, if this is the first time you are hearing of such wizardry, allow me to break down what the three-point formula is.

1. Exercise

It sounds obvious, it sounds simple, but so many people are not exercising their dog nearly enough. So many problems can arise when your dog is not getting a release for all that pent-up energy. Just like with people, exercise is a key component towards a healthy, balanced lifestyle. Now before I talk about what proper exercise is, it is worth noting that exercise requirements will differ from dog to dog, depending on age, breed, health, etc. For example, a greyhound might be the fastest dog on the planet, but it doesn't actually require as much exercise as you may think. In fact, 45 minutes–1 hour a day is often more than adequate for a breed coined 'the world's fastest couch potato'! That being said, a Belgian Malinois – in my view, the terminator of dog breeds, a through and through working breed – would likely develop a whole host of behavioural issues if they were given the same exercise daily as a greyhound. For a healthy adult dog, 1–2 hours of exercise a day is generally an ideal amount.

So what is proper exercise? Proper exercise consists of three main things: physical, mental and breed-specific exercise. These three elements will often overlap, but including all of them on a daily basis is very important, especially when you are out on walks.

Physical exercise

Physical exercise is just that: it is when the dog is doing something physical such as going for a walk, chasing a tennis ball or playing with another dog. It is something that gets the heart pumping, the joints moving and the muscles working. When we talk about physical exercise, it is important to mix it up so as not to create issues in their behaviour or health. For example, on a Monday you may choose to go for a nice stroll with your dog, a casual walk in which you let the dog have a good old sniff along the way. Tuesday you may decide to head down to your local park and play fetch. It is important not to do the same thing every single day. Mix it up each day so that these activities do not become an expectation or an obsession.

Mental stimulation

Mental stimulation is something that gets the brain working, gets those cogs turning, and your dog thinking. Mental stimulation should be combined, where possible, with physical exercise. Examples of mental stimulation could be adding some basic obedience (see p. 36) before throwing a ball for your dog. Or you could even add some basic commands at random parts on a good old-fashioned lead walk. Mental stimulation can also be games such as 'Find it', which is where you hide, for example, your dog's favourite treats. One of the best and easiest forms of mental stimulation is taking your dog somewhere new and getting them to use their nose to sniff and explore. Remember, guys, dogs are scent-driven animals; every time your dog is sniffing, it is the equivalent to you going on Google and searching for information. The dog takes in all of this information through scent; it's natural, it's enriching, it's calming and, best of all, it's tiring. So by combining physical and mental exercise, you are really getting the best out of your dog.

Breed-specific fulfilment

Now the final part of proper exercise overlaps with both physical and mental exercise, but is more geared towards what your dog was designed to do, what they were bred for. There is no coincidence that the Springer Spaniel and the Great Dane are two completely different dogs with completely different temperaments, personalities, energy levels and skillsets. Although they are both dogs, selective breeding has meant nearly all dogs were bred to have unique traits.

Understanding what your dog was designed to do and what they were bred for will help you with your training. You can incorporate some of this into your dog's day-to-day life. If we know that Labradors love to retrieve, there is a strong possibility that incorporating that into our training is going to be extremely rewarding. If we know that spaniels love to search, then giving them something to find is going to be a winner for them.

Now some dogs were bred for stuff that we can't incorporate into our day-to-day life, like bull baiting or dog fighting, and quite rightly so. However, this doesn't mean we can't find an outlet for these genetic behaviours and the smashmouth style of play that some of these breeds may exhibit. I find exercises like tug-of-war combined with some obedience to be a great outlet for this physical style of dogs.

Sometimes you may not necessarily know what your dog was designed to do, and that's okay; many times if you just listen to your dog, it will tell us what it wants to do. You may find that it is an avid sniffer, or constantly brings you stuff, or likes toys. You just need to listen and observe what your dog is naturally trying to do and then, where possible, incorporate that into your training. And don't forget that all dogs are scent-driven, and nearly all dogs love food and fuss and interaction from their owner, so any way of incorporating this into your training routine is a win.

So that's exercise in a nutshell. Get this bit right and you will have a much happier dog, and a happy dog is a happy life!

2. The off switch

One of the biggest issues I see these days, one that contributes to so many anxiety-based behaviour issues in dogs, is the dog's inability to switch off and settle down. Dogs are meant to sleep for 16–18 hours a day, but most dogs that have behavioural problems are not coming close to that. Now if your dog doesn't switch off, it can develop problems such excessive barking, separation anxiety, destructive behaviour, etc.

If you combine this with a newborn baby, life will get stressful very quickly. When you have a newborn baby, they are going to need plenty of naps. That's completely normal and I think we all understand this. But, for some reason, when it comes to dogs, we don't take this into consideration and it even holds true for ourselves – not enough downtime and relaxation can cause all sorts of stress.

So how can we help dogs switch off? It is actually easier than you may think. If you are exercising your dog enough and then put it in its crate after exercise for a minimum of 2 hours, then your dog will learn to calm down, relax and decompress after exercise. We go into detail about crate training later on (see pp. 43–5) and how it can help you, especially when you have a baby or toddler. By utilising the crate after exercise and adrenaline-based activities, you will eventually be able to come away from the crate and your dog will just naturally settle.

My little rescue Mila no longer needs a crate and after a good walk will just hop onto the sofa on her blanket and go to sleep.

3. Diet

The final point to the three-point formula that is often overlooked and not given much thought when it comes to dogs is the food that we feed them on a daily basis. A poor diet can contribute to health and even behavioural problems.

Before I knew any better, I would just feed what I saw on television, such as the dried biscuit brands (we don't need to name them), believing this was the best for my dog. But my late staffie Sammie used to get blocked anal glands almost on a monthly basis. This would make her very defensive when other dogs would go to sniff her, which was completely uncharacteristic of a dog that was so sociable the rest of the time. The reason for her defensiveness was because she was uncomfortable. When a dog is uncomfortable or in pain, they can behave completely out of character. I later discovered that it was her diet that was causing her anal glands to be blocked. So you can see how diet can play a big part in helping behaviour-related issues.

The diet I feed my dogs now, and the diet I will always feed my dogs, is a raw food diet. In my opinion, and in the opinion of many nutritionists, it is the best diet for a dog. When I put Sammie on a raw food diet, she never got blocked anal glands again. In the past thirteen years of working with dogs, I have seen raw food help countless dogs not just in behaviour-related issues, but health issues too. You can read more about a raw food diet by visiting our website www.southenddogtraining.co.uk.

It is important to note that a raw food diet does require extra care and consideration, because, as the name suggests, you are handling raw meat, so with young children around it is important to take extra care and precautions with regard to hygiene.

Of course, raw food is not for everyone, and that's okay! So here are a couple of things to look out for when trying to determine what makes good dog food.

A good alternative to raw food is cold-pressed dog food (widely available in the UK or via our website). It has many similar health benefits to raw food, but is similar to kibble or dry food in texture. Unlike kibble, cold-pressed food is cooked at much lower temperatures, which helps to maintain the good nutrients.

But whatever food you choose, the first ingredient listed on the packaging is the most important, and that ingredient must be a meat, and not a meat derivative. You also want to make sure it does not contain too many unnecessary ingredients, such as sugars. You do not have to be nutritionist to know whether it is good or bad; a quick search on Google will tell you all you need to know. The same way you don't need to be a health expert to understand that fast food as a main staple of your diet is not good for you.

So that's it when it comes to the three-point formula. Getting this right can help prevent so many problems with your dog, and if your dog does have problems, it can begin to make life much easier all round, which will in turn make raising a newborn much easier. Now let's talk about some other things that your dog needs to know before the new arrival.

COMMANDS

Commands are pretty self-explanatory; they are literally something you ask your dog to do. So what commands are important and how do we teach them?

The 'Sit' command

This is one of the first basic and useful commands to teach – but be aware that 'Sit' must mean sit. Sit is so much more than just the action. It's the ability to hold that command until released, no matter what is going on. It can keep your dog calm and safe. If your dog can sit and hold that sit, you can use it to help with dogs that lunge. You can use it to help with jumping up too, and we will delve into this in more detail in later chapters. You will see how important this command is as we dig into more serious behaviour issues.

And remember, if you've asked your dog to sit and you haven't released it from that position or given further instructions and it isn't still in that sit, you're not being consistent. That dog had better go back into that sit!

How to teach 'Sit'

With a treat in your fingers, hold it to your dog's nose and slowly raise it above the dog's head. As the dog's head comes up, their bum naturally comes down. Once this happens, wait for them to make eye contact, say 'Yes' as the marker word and then step back and give the dog the treat.

When this command is understood, you can move on to using the duration marker of 'Good', returning to the dog to reward it after you use the 'Good' marker. Build the duration of sit by using the 'Good' marker and taking one additional step further back each time. Bit by bit, as your dog is waiting for 'Good' and the reward, the sit duration is increasing.

When the distance you have achieved with 'Good' is suitable, use the 'Sit' command, wait for eye contact and you can instead use the marker word 'Yes', which will release the dog to come to you for the reward instead.

The 'Down' command

Just like 'Sit', the 'Down' command is so important and, just like 'Sit', the stay in down is implied. A dog must hold that down until released or given further instructions.

If your dog can obey 'Down' anywhere, anytime, regardless of situation or distraction, you can take your dog virtually anywhere dogs are permitted. It will help them in pubs, restaurants and at friends' houses. You can use it to help a dog settle down. 'Down' is so powerful if you are consistent with it. But remember, 'Down' means down until given further instructions.

How to teach 'Down'

With a treat in your fingers, hold it to your dog's nose and slowly bring the treat to the floor, until they are on the floor too. If you need to get their bum down that final bit, move the treat towards you. The moment all four legs and bum are down, say 'Yes' and reward your dog with the treat. Repeat this to reinforce the command.

To increase duration for 'Down', use your 'Good' marker to build up time, just as you did with 'Sit'. When you have achieved a reasonable 'Down' duration, work in the 'Yes' marker so that the dog can come to you for the treat.

As you can see, 'Sit' and 'Down' are very similar in the way they are taught. The way to add distance and duration is the same, and the same for distraction. In my experience, 'Down' is slightly more difficult for the dog to master than 'Sit', but that doesn't mean you should brush past it. I would typically use 'Down' for duration work, i.e. if I needed the dog to hold a position for a longer period of time, and use 'Sit' for shorter scenarios.

Indirect recall

The best way to describe indirect recall would be when you say something along the lines of, 'Mila, this way'. This would apply when your dog is wandering off and you just want it to come with you in your direction. Indirect recall means your dog doesn't have to come all the way to you, he just has to stay close and follow your direction. I always teach indirect recall first because it makes that direct recall much easier.

When I teach indirect recall, I put the dog on a long line (BioThane long lines are great for this) and when the dog wanders too far in front of me, I change direction and say, 'This way' and guide the dog back in my direction. I repeat the above many times, changing direction often.

The beauty of indirect recall is that you have probably been using this already on lead walks or over fields without even realising it, and, on the whole, it is easier for a lot of dogs to get. This one also means that the dog is paying more attention to you, because you are unpredictable when you keep changing direction. When a dog needs to pay attention to you, it's automatically listening to you too. This now makes it easier to teach direct recall.

Direct recall

This is probably the recall command you'll be expecting to use. Direct recall means when you call 'Come', you expect your dog to come all the way to you and wait for a release from the command, rather than just carrying on in your general direction, doing whatever it was doing.

In the beginning, when your dog has returned to you at the 'Come' command, it's important to reward it every time, to drum home what you want. The reward could be a toy, food or fuss, or even just letting the dog go straight back out after coming back to you so the environment itself is the reward, if you have an avid sniffer. The main thing to remember is that if you use direct recall, you must make sure you release your dog afterwards.

At SDT we recommend practising both types of recall in conjunction with each other. This is because indirect recall means your dog is paying attention, and that's a great time to reinforce direct recall. Use both types of recall randomly for the best results rather than a week of one and then a week of the other.

If you're struggling, try stripping it all back and ask yourself what the problem might be. Do you need to find a quieter place? Are you working too fast for your dog? Do you need to up your rewards or try something easier? Make your training sessions fun until motivation comes back.

Jumping up

Jumping up is one of the most common issues we see with pet dogs. Some people may find it cute, particularly if they have a smaller dog. However, you are the one that sets the tone; if the dog can do it to you, it most certainly could attempt to do it to a child. As an adult, you are obviously much bigger than a small child, so a dog jumping up at you may seem innocent and cute, but when it scratches or knocks over your child and your child is now kicking and screaming, you're not going to find this so cute.

So how do we stop jumping up? You need to make sure that the dog is on a lead inside the house for this exercise. I recommend an indoor training line: this is thin and lightweight and is designed to go under door frames and not snag on furniture. The reason 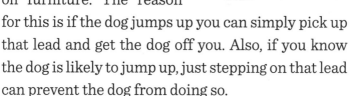 for this is if the dog jumps up you can simply pick up that lead and get the dog off you. Also, if you know the dog is likely to jump up, just stepping on that lead can prevent the dog from doing so.

You also want to get into the habit of teaching your dog to sit before you stroke it. After all, dogs jump up because it gets them attention. They normally learn this behaviour when they are puppies, when they are small and especially cute, so you need to make sure that the dog is sitting before you stroke it in the beginning. As the dog approaches, simply ask it to sit and ensure it is in a sit before stroking it. If the dog goes to jump up, simply take hold of its lead and lead it off you. Repeat until the dog understands what you are asking of them.

A couple of things to bear in mind: dogs often jump up when they are excited and because it gets them attention. So if you have a dog that jumps up you must be aware that the more excited you are when stroking or interacting with it, the more likely the dog is to jump up. You need to practise calm interactions with your dog when working on this. You also need to make sure that you are not sending mixed messages by stroking the dog as it jumps up before leading them off as this will confuse the dog. Consistency here is key; be patient and don't get frustrated.

So remember, indoor training lead on, and drum into your dog 'Sit', stroke, 'Sit', stroke. It is very important in the beginning that when you are stroking the dog, you stroke them very calmly, almost as if you are giving them a nice head massage. You need to teach them that all four paws on the floor means stroke, affection, reward.

I also recommend you get a life-size baby doll and practise carrying this around with you, ensuring that you can control the dog while holding your pretend baby. It might feel strange at first, and although your dog knows it is not a real baby, the act of practising while holding a doll can prepare you better for when you have the real thing.

You should also practise walking towards your dog, holding the baby and giving the dog a treat if all four paws are on the floor. This will help teach the dog that all four paws on the floor means good things are coming and it will make it less likely to jump up.

CRATE TRAINING

Crate training is something that will be an absolute game-changer for your dog, especially when you have a newborn baby on the scene. In my opinion, every single dog on the planet should be crate-trained.

Video on crate training:

Crate training isn't sticking your dog in prison. It's not putting them in there as punishment; it is providing a safe space for your dog they can retreat to when life is stressful. It's a den-like environment if you will, but it's also somewhere you can put the dog after or during certain activities to teach them how to behave. Imagine a crate as a cot for your dog. Your baby will be going into a cot and your baby will have regular naps. A crate is a cot for a dog. Ideally, it is introduced in puppyhood to enforce regular nap times so your dog learns to relax, settle and switch off, but it can be used at any age and introduced at any age.

Why do I encourage crate training for all dog owners? Crate training can help with a whole host of issues – a lot of anxiety-based behaviours such as excessive barking, destruction and separation anxiety to name just a few. These are often symptomatic of a dog that isn't getting enough exercise or is getting enough exercise but doesn't know how to switch off. This kind of dog is constantly up, down, up, down like a yoyo, constantly having broken sleep. They are never fully decompressing and this can lead to anxiety.

When you start crate training, we recommend using it at these times:

After exercise

A lot of dogs get enough exercise but struggle to switch off, so are constantly on the go. By crating your dog after exercise for a minimum of 2 hours your dog can learn to decompress and switch off. What this leads to over time is your dog being much more relaxed and content, and this will make your life much easier.

Food time

Along with crating your dog after exercise, you need to crate your dog any time food is being prepared or eaten, whether by you, the baby or your guests. So many dogs steal food, or sit there begging for food, which can become problematic, especially when a baby begins to wave food around as they normally do. A dog could try to exploit this and take it from the baby. It can confuse the dog when babies or toddlers wave food around. It is almost like teasing them; this unintentional act exhibited by the child can lead to the dog trying its luck and potentially taking something it shouldn't and can cause it to nip the child by accident when trying to take the food from their hand. In turn, this can actually become a fun game for the child, exacerbating the problem.

When I first got Mila, my rescue dog, any time food was being prepared or eaten we'd put her in her crate. She remained there until the food was finished, and as long as she was calm, we let her out of the crate. If there was a bit of food left over that was safe for her to eat, we would use that as a reward for staying in her crate nicely. Now Mila doesn't have to be told to go in her crate when there is food; she automatically gets off the sofa and goes straight into her crate when food comes outs. We don't ever have to close the crate door because it is now a default behaviour for her. She knows that it is rewarding for her to go there, and as a result we do not have any issues with food.

You are going to be feeding your baby a lot and when that baby becomes a toddler, which we get into later (see Chapter 6), it is going to be messy – there will often be food everywhere, on the floors, walls, even ceilings. It happens! Having your dog understand what is expected of them will just make your life – and theirs – that little bit easier.

How to crate train

To start crate training, you'll need your dog's favourite treats. Show them the treats and get them interested. Throw some treats deep into the crate and say 'Crate' so the dog follows the food in, snuffles to find the treats, and then, when the dog's attention returns to you, use a marker word such as 'Yes' for the dog to come out again and receive another treat. Your aim to is get your dog to go happily into the crate.

Do this over and over, keeping it rewarding for your dog, and then gradually build up the time the dog is in the crate. Work up to closing the door between the dog going in and coming out, and then to walking away out of the room too. The key here is to build a positive association with the crate in your dog's head. That's why you need to work on it as if it's a training game. You can also feed your dog through the bars of the crate when they are inside to increase the feel-good factor.

It's also important to ensure a calm exit, so only open the crate door if the dog is calm (not rushing). For an overexcited dog, consider popping them on a lead as they come out. A lead can be useful to encourage a reluctant dog into the crate too.

Crate training is non-negotiable, so make sure this fun game of in/out is one of the first things you tackle.

Quick crate hack

If your dog doesn't settle when in the crate, a good hack is to cover the crate with a blanket but leave a small 'window' at the bottom of it. This means your dog has to lie down to be able to see out, and once it is lying down, it's instantly more relaxed.

Desensitising your dog to baby's crying

This is by far one of the most important things you need to do because babies cry – a lot. And often when babies cry, it can be quite a stressful experience. We are often sleep deprived at these times and, as a new parent, it can be worrying if we don't quite know how to settle the baby; the last thing we want is a dog that is unsettled at this time, adding to the stress. Dogs can also often find a small infant crying quite a stressful ordeal. I am going to discuss how to prepare the dog for your new arrival crying, so that the dog doesn't find it stressful, and we are also going to teach the dog what is expected of them when the baby is crying so that they know what to do.

Before your baby's arrival, I recommend playing sound clips of babies crying from YouTube or other sources. This can be a good way of getting the dog used to the sound of babies crying. At this time, send the dog to its crate and shut the door, then go over to your pretend baby, pick it up, turn off the sound of the baby crying, go over to the crate and give the dog a treat. Put the baby back down and then release the dog from its crate, providing the dog is in a calm state of mind. You'll need to practise this randomly throughout the day in different rooms, and for different durations.

By doing this, you are teaching the dog what is expected of them when the baby is crying. This helps the dog to relax because they have clear instructions and a clear understanding. It will make your life easier when the baby is crying because now you won't have to worry about the dog; you can just concentrate on your baby.

Hopefully by now you are starting to see that in order to make your life and your dog's life easier, you have to teach the dog what is expected of them before the baby has even arrived. So when you are dealing with a real baby, none of this is foreign to your dog.

How To Raise The Perfect Family Dog

Changing the baby's nappy

Now this is usually the part where I would make a naughty joke, along with potentially throwing in a swear word; however, this is a family-friendly book, so let's go with a lame old dad joke and say, 'this subject stinks'. As a parent of three children,

I have changed my fair share of nappies and, I will be honest with you, it never gets better. But there is nothing worse than having a dog invading your personal space, trying to climb on you, getting their nose too close to that dirty nappy as you are trying to change your baby. So, let's get practising with our pretend baby.

While holding the pretend baby, you are going to send your dog to its crate. Get your changing mat out and all the other bits that come with it – the baby wipes, talc powder, lotions, etc. – these are important to this exercise. They all have unique smells to them, so getting your dog desensitised to these smells will help them to understand that when these items come out, it is crate time. With the dog in its crate, pretend to change the baby's nappy. When you've finished, head back to the crate, along with a reward, and let the dog out, giving them lots of praise.

Breastfeeding

The same method can be applied to breastfeeding. Breastfeeding is a very emotional bonding experience, and sometimes it can be challenging. Now, I'm not going to claim to be an expert on this subject, for obvious reasons. But I can, however, tell you that teaching your dog what to do before the baby arrives will ensure things go a lot smoother for you. If you are not breastfeeding, you can apply the same principles.

Now, you may be thinking that we are using the crate a lot, and will this be a forever thing. At the end of this chapter, I will talk to you about how to come away from the crate and use a specific place and/or spot on the sofa instead that the dog will go to, so fear not.

Rules for the sofa and bed

Depending on who you ask, everybody has their own opinion on this subject: should your dog be allowed on the sofa, should they not be allowed on the sofa? The reality is, it is your personal preference. I love having a cuddle with my dogs in the evening on the sofa. My two dogs Mila and Roxy are absolute snuggle monsters, not just with me, but also with my wife and children. It melts my heart every single time when one of my children gets a blanket out, puts the TV on and snuggles with the dogs. But there have to be rules, especially with small children in the house.

My cardinal rule – and this is non-negotiable – is if your dog guards the sofa or bed, or people on the sofa or bed, it does not have those privileges. In Chapter 4 we dig deeper into this behavioural problem.

One of the behaviours that I teach dogs is they have to be invited onto the sofa; they cannot just jump onto the sofa whenever they feel like it, just because you have sat down. Remember how I said earlier that certain behaviours may not seem problematic?

If your dog can jump on the sofa and all over you just because you have sat down, imagine what can happen when you are sitting down with the baby in your arms. It is important that you can sit down and get yourself comfortable before inviting the dog onto the sofa.

Now I know some of you will already be in the position where your dog jumps up onto the sofa or bed like I have just described. So how can you reverse this? With the dog on its indoor training lead, sit on the sofa with your pretend baby. If the dog jumps up you simply lead it off the sofa. If the dog does this ten times you lead them off the sofa ten times. What you are waiting for is for the dog to stop jumping on the sofa without you first inviting them, and instead having the dog wait for you to invite them up.

Do not stroke the dog or interact with the dog in any way until it is calm and settled on the sofa. Any behaviour you don't like, simply remove the dog from the sofa and repeat the previous step.

I have never been one for using props in dog training. I am a huge advocate for real-world dog training. If I am working with a dog and they do not like other people, I will use real people. If I am working with a dog that doesn't like other dogs, then I won't use a stuffed dog; I will use a real, living, breathing dog that is highly trained to help with the training. But when it comes to practising these exercises in preparation for a baby that is not yet here, using a pretend baby is the closest thing you can do to prepare yourself and the dog for the real thing. Getting your reps in now will make a world of difference for when the baby arrives.

The last thing I like to teach is that if a dog is on the sofa and I am holding the baby, as I approach the sofa, the dog gets off. This will help with the dog having to wait for an invitation, but as the dog progresses in its training this will help it become a default behaviour. As people walk towards the sofa, the dog gets off, which in turn will allow you, your children or your guests to get a nice spot on the sofa and get comfortable. Then, if they wish to, they can invite the dog onto the sofa.

For me, it's not about whether the dog is or isn't allowed on the sofa; it's about whether or not you have the option to have the dog on the sofa. It's about making sure the dog is respectful on the sofa (or bed) and understands the rules around them.

How To Raise The Perfect Family Dog

Leave it

This has made an appearance in all three of my books because it is one of the most important commands you will ever teach your dog, regardless of having children or not. 'Leave it' is pretty self-explanatory: it simply means that if I want the dog not to go near something or to drop an item, I say 'Leave it' and I expect the dog to leave it alone.

So why is this important and how does it apply to having a child and a dog? Well, it's important because it can literally be the difference between life and death. Think about it like this: if your dog picks up something that it shouldn't, whether that is inside the house or outside, and you cannot get them to leave it, what would happen if that item was hazardous to your dog's health? For instance, a smashed snow globe – did you know that most snow globes contain anti-freeze, which if your dog ingests it, can be fatal?

'Leave it', however, is something that we are likely to use a lot in our day-to-day lives, but will also come up around children's toys. Many children's toys are very similar to dog toys – they are small, plastic, and they jangle and squeak! You obviously don't want your baby and dog to share the same toys, not least because both babies and dogs like to put things in their mouths.

So how do we teach 'Leave it'? I use two different methods. One is with the dog on a lead and items on the floor; the other is through playing tug or fetch. I like the second method best as the dog has a toy in its mouth, but both methods cover both scenarios where the dog might have to leave something that's on the ground or already in its mouth.

Leave it: Method one

First, you'll need an everyday item your dog is not allowed. A kids' toy is a great example, maybe even a cuddly one that resembles a small furry animal, as it's very tempting.

Before you start, ensure your dog is on a training lead. Show it the toy, then take the toy and throw it a short distance away from your dog where it can still be seen. The dog's natural curiosity will mean it wants to go over and investigate. Use the lead to gently prevent this and say 'Leave it' when the lead goes slack, and use the marker 'Yes' to reinforce that the dog has done as asked when it is no longer pulling. The dog has effectively stopped trying to reach the toy and you should reward this. I recommend you practise this a lot with different items in different rooms at different times to ensure the dog accepts the command and that it applies to every situation, and not just a particular one such as that specific toy, or that room at that time, etc.

Leave it: Method two

This is another way to teach the 'Leave it' command. I use a tug toy – something the dog can bite on and play with. I like to get the dog chasing the rope a bit and then let them grab it, have a right old tug and then stop the game completely. Make sure you say 'Leave it' as you are holding the toy and stop tugging it so that the game becomes boring. When the dog releases the toy, let them get straight back onto the toy and the fun begins again. You can repeat this method over and over until it is fluid. If your dog is more ball-orientated, then use the two-ball method: throw one ball and, as the dog comes back with the ball in its mouth, present ball number two and use the 'Leave it' command. This nearly always gets the dog to drop the ball they have. Then throw the second ball and repeat. Practise this method at random times, just as you did with method one.

Lead walking

Lead walking is super important to teach any dog. Teaching them how to walk nicely on a lead makes walks enjoyable for them, but also for yourself. Now having a dog that can come on adventures

How To Raise The Perfect Family Dog

with you and your newborn baby means everybody can be involved. But often we have to leave the dog behind when we have a newborn because pushing a pram with a dog that is pulling can quickly become problematic.

Many times the dog's routine can change a little bit when we have a baby, and it can be difficult to find time to exercise them, so being able to take the dog and baby out at the same time is a great way of making sure the dog still gets regular daily exercise. So let's talk more about lead walking and why it is beneficial.

Lead walking is one of the most powerful exercises you can do with your dog. When it's done correctly it can reduce many behavioural issues and improve other areas such as recall and attention. Correct lead walking can build confidence in a nervous dog, slow down an anxious mind and provide clarity all round. But lead walking is so much more than just attaching a lead and setting off on your way; it's a partnership, a bonding exercise and a calming mental exercise. If there's one thing that nearly every dog you'll meet shares, it is that they all needed work at some point to walk nicely on a lead.

Now while I said that lead walking builds a relationship between you and your dog, you should also know that it's not a 50–50 relationship. It's more like a parent–child relationship, with the dog being the child. It's so important that you have rules in place, and that it's structured, but it must also be fun for the dog. We will cover those rules in a moment.

Give and take

A lot of trainers believe that the walk is for the dog so you should let it do whatever it wants, but this is very harmful advice. While I agree the walk is for the dog, it is also for you. It's no good if the dog is having the time of its life, but you are having your arm pulled out of its socket. It's also no good if the dog is hyper-aroused, nervous or reacting to everything: this isn't going to be enjoyable for you or your dog.

Letting a dog have too much freedom and making all the choices will often lead to more problems down the line. Dogs need structure, but not in the 'I as your owner, must be pack leader' way. I don't agree with that either. That mindset leads to the type of walk where the dog is forced to walk by your side or behind you, where he must follow your every move, isn't allowed to sniff and isn't ever allowed in front. This approach is boring and unnecessary. What we're aiming for is balance, a give and take.

My idea of a good walk would be that the dog walks nicely by your side for 10–15 minutes, at your pace, doing as you ask, with you setting the tone. If you stop, the dog stops. If you speed up, the dog speeds up. But then, as a reward for a job well done, you ask the dog to sit, wait for eye contact and then release the dog to be in front. This is now your dog's time to explore further. If they stop, you can stop. If they stay there too long, you can usher them on, but it's now the dog's time. You do this for 5–10 minutes then go back to structure, and you keep going back and forth between this. It's very important though, that whether the dog is in front of you or by your side, it's not pulling.

What side should the dog walk on?

Primarily when teaching a 'Heel', we put the dog on the left side. But, unless you are planning on competing with your dog, choosing which side of you your dog walks is more a personal preference. Choose whichever side you feel comfortable with. There is no scientific evidence to support the idea that dogs walk better on the left or the right. So, you do what's best for you and your dog. If you're going to use both sides at some point, I'd recommend using a different command for left and right, i.e. 'Heel' for your left side and 'Close' for your right.

Which training tools should you use?

To begin with, I like to use a regular collar and a front clip harness with a double-ended lead. I attach one of the ends of the lead to the dog's collar and the other end to the dog's front clip on the harness. This combination allows me to control both body and head. This is a great set-up for mild pullers.

At SDT we tend not to use harnesses alone on dogs that pull. The reason for this is simple: harnesses for the best part are designed so the dog can pull comfortably. And all dogs know how to pull! General excitement, and the fact they have four legs while we only have two, means they often move faster than us. A harness makes pulling much easier and gives more of the control to the dog. You can, of course, use a harness to teach a dog to walk nicely, but it's going to take so much longer than necessary. Instead, using a harness with a collar means you can have full control and can steer the dog where you want them. It also means that if the dog is really pulling, the combination of the two takes a lot of pressure off the throat, so no choking. This harness-and-collar combo can be used right from the first walk.

For big pullers I would maybe consider something like a Halti or Dogmatic. These are headcollars that give you much more control. If you use a Halti though, it's important that you take the time to condition your dog to it, so it's comfortable wearing one. To do this, scan the below QR code and enter the password SDTBook to gain access to the video.

What is a Halti?

A Halti can be used once a dog reaches six months of age. The Halti headcollar was invented over thirty years ago and is a bit like a halter worn by horses. Also known as a gentle leader or head halter, the Halti basically goes over the dog's head, with the bigger loop going around the back of the head and the smaller loop going over the dog's muzzle (as shown in the image). A correctly worn Halti should provide enough space to allow one finger to slide under the cheek strap, meaning it won't interfere with panting, eating or drinking.

Slip leads

Slip leads are another tool I use a lot as they're great for controlling the dog and for teaching pressure. This is because, if a slip lead is fitted correctly, it sits snugly right at the top of a dog's neck and distributes any pressure equally. This is not like a normal collar, which puts all the pressure at the base of the throat. This allows for better communication with your dog. However, the slip lead itself doesn't stop the dog pulling and nor will any tool. The tool is simply an aid; you have to teach the dog what it means. No matter what tool you use it's important that it's used correctly.

How to begin lead walking

The first thing to remember is that your dog should *always* be calm at the start of the walk. Don't say,

'Do you want to go walkies?' Of course the dog wants to go for a walk! All you're doing by saying this is creating a precursor for excitement and encouraging your dog to go mental. Excitement will make pulling more likely.

You also want to make sure the dog doesn't go mental simply at the sight of the lead. To avoid this, pick up the lead you use for walking regularly throughout the day and move it, even when you're not going on a walk. You might get some initial excitement as the dog thinks the lead always means walkies, but quickly the dog will realise you picking up the lead is just that. The association between you picking up a lead and then going for a walk will be broken.

When it is time for the walk, call your dog to you and attach the lead. If the dog goes crazy, sit down for a minute and wait for the dog to calm down. When the dog is calm, go to the front door. But before you open the door, make sure that the dog is behind you and not in front of you – you should be between the dog and the door, and the dog should be in a sit. Next, open the door. If the dog comes out of the sit, shut the door and reset. Repeat until you can get the door open and the dog is sitting nicely behind you.

When you have eye contact, lead the dog through the front door or say 'Heel' if your dog knows that command; don't say 'Okay', 'Break' or 'Go on then'. These are often words that mean the dog can go run and play and is essentially free, so this will undo what you want. You want a calm dog ahead of the walk. As soon as you are outside, get the dog back into a sit (remember sit means sit) and shut the front door.

If you follow the above instructions, you're starting the walk the right way straight away, and you will see a massive difference. If you don't start in the right way, like most people, you'll fail the walk before it's even begun. Don't worry if following the advice at the start of the walk takes a long time. This approach is a mental exercise, which is draining, but what takes a long time today will get shorter and easier each day *if* you are consistent. Then you'll have years of calm walks ahead of you both.

Pro tips

I recommend you practise auto stops, or what we at SDT call 'applying the brakes'. To do this, every few minutes or so and for no reason, gently pull up on the lead and come to a stop and pop the dog in a sit. You want the dog to learn that any time you stop, whether it's because you have to or just because, the dog is to go into a sit. This will help massively if you have a reactive dog on the lead. Just bear in mind that some dogs, like sighthounds, have trouble sitting comfortably because of their anatomy, while older dogs may be arthritic. If this is the case for your dog, try asking for a 'Stop' position instead. (If your dog is struggling to sit and you don't know why, a visit to the vet might be in order.)

Another thing to make sure you are doing is holding the lead, short but relaxed, by your side. The lead should have just enough slack in it so that when your dog is by your side there is no tension, but as soon as the dog goes rogue and starts to go in front, you feel that tension and you gently pull up. Pulling up slows the dog down. Don't pull back though, as pulling back often creates an opposition reflex and makes a dog pull more.

Lead walking with a pram

Having your dog walking nicely is great, but having it walk nicely next to a pram, that's the real game changer. Nailing this will ensure that you will be able to include your dog and baby on little adventures together. This will also help kill two birds with one stone, as you will be exercising your dog and getting the baby some fresh air. So how do we go about this?

Ensure basic lead training

Before introducing the pram, ensure your dog has basic lead training and understands what is expected of them on the lead. Follow all the advice above.

Familiarise your dog with the pram

Start by letting your dog sniff and investigate the pram in a safe, controlled environment. Allow your dog to get accustomed to the sights, sounds and smells of the pram before attempting to walk with it. I would start by just having the pram out in the living room or hallway, or wherever is practical for a few days, before doing anything else. The next step, if the dog is comfortable, would be just to push the pram around the house or garden a little bit, not making a big deal out of this.

DON'T FORGET TO REWARD YOUR DOG!

Use treats and praise to create positive associations with the pram. Give treats and praise whenever your dog shows calm behaviour around the pram, such as sitting or standing calmly next to it.

Introduce the pram on walks

When you know your dog is comfortable with the sight and movement of the pram, it is now time to begin getting your dog to walk nicely alongside it. You need to practise this before the baby is even here. Start in your garden and then move onto the streets, starting in areas with a low level of distractions.

Reward your dog with treats and praise them for walking calmly and staying close to the pram.

Keep the lead short enough to maintain control over your dog, but with enough slack to allow them to walk comfortably.

If your dog starts to pull or becomes overly excited, use gentle lead corrections and redirect their attention back to you.

Practise walking with the pram and your dog regularly to reinforce good behaviour and build consistency.

Always supervise interactions between your dog and the pram to ensure the safety of both your dog and your baby, and be prepared to intervene if your dog shows signs of anxiety or aggression around the pram.

By following these steps and being patient and consistent, you can teach your dog to walk calmly next to a pram, allowing you to enjoy walks with your baby safely and comfortably. Remember to always prioritise the safety and wellbeing of both your dog and your baby during training sessions.

How To Raise The Perfect Family Dog

Moving on from the crate

This is likely your final goal, but it's not necessarily an age thing. It's more about judging when it's safe for your dog to be given the run of the house/room. If your dog is toilet trained, knows how to settle when the baby is around and is not destructive in any way, then it's likely ready for a bit more freedom.

Some dogs may never be ready. My late dog Sammie was still crated when we left the house. There are several reasons: one is that she loved to chew Barbie dolls, which my kids love to leave out; and the other is that she didn't like loud bangs, which we have locally. She instinctively felt safer in her crate because of this. Roxy, my other dog, by comparison, is not crated when we leave. Different dogs, different needs. Either way, it's a mistake to stop using the crate too soon, so don't rush that.

A good way of transitioning away from the crate is to begin to teach a command we like to call 'Place'. So what is 'Place'?

'Place' is basically a spot you can send the dog to, for example a bed, where you want your dog to stay and settle. It is similar to the crate, but it doesn't have a door. The good thing about 'Place' is once you have taught it using the dog's bed, for instance, you can then use a different place, i.e. a blanket on the sofa or a mat on the floor that you can then send the dog to. Eventually 'Place' becomes a universal command to stay in that said place. So how do we teach this?

How to teach 'Place'

'Place' is very simple to teach. It is not so dissimilar to crate training, but a lot more consistency is needed – you will see why in a minute. The first thing to do is to get a comfortable dog bed  or a mat and put it in your designated spot. Then leave it there for a few days. Sometimes the dog may naturally go straight over to it to investigate or, better still, just lie on it (this is a win!). If this happens, be sure to reward your dog. After a few days your dog should be more than comfortable with the new bed in the house, so now it is time to teach the dog how to go there and stay there on command. This is how you do it.

With the dog on its lead, walk over to the bed and lead the dog onto it. As soon as all four paws are on the bed, reward your dog. Then lead them straight off the bed using your release word. Repeat this process several times until the dog is comfortable doing so. When you sense that the dog is comfortable and has the hang of this game, repeat the above, but add a command this time.

It should look a little like this: hold the dog's lead, walk towards the bed, say 'Place' and lead the dog onto the bed. Once all four paws are in the place, reward your dog. It is at this stage that you begin to ask for some duration. Repeat the steps but then count to 3 seconds before giving them the release command. Then move up to 5 and then 10 seconds.

It is important that if your dog comes off the designated place before you have released them, you put them straight back on, but you do not reward them for going back. I'll explain why shortly. Consistency is now going to come into effect. If your dog gets off the place ten times without permission, it goes back ten times, because it's important that your dog understands that 'Place' means 'Place' until they are released or given further instructions. As with your baby, you are going to need eyes in the back of your head when teaching this, as inconsistencies here will lead to a more wilful, stubborn dog. But stubbornness is bred through inconsistent communication.

Why don't we reward the dog if it breaks position and we have to put them back in that position? I'll put it into language that should resonate with parents-to-be. It is a bit like asking your children to wash up, they say 'No', and you then offer them a fiver to wash up. You have effectively bribed your child. Your child in this moment will learn to ignore you next time, because it literally pays to do so. The same principle applies for dogs. Now you can say to your children that if they do their chores that you are going to reward them with pocket money, and it is the same again for dogs. If I send you to your place or ask you to do something, I will pay you for a job well done. But if you ignore me, you are not getting paid. Now because dogs have got short attention spans, if the dog comes off its place and you have to put the dog back on its place because you haven't released it, after a few seconds or minutes, if the dog is still on there, you may go over and reward them, to let them know you are happy with what they are doing.

The simplest way of remembering this is if you ask the dog to do something and they do it at the first time of asking, they get paid. If you have to repeat yourself because the dog isn't listening, there is no reward and you make it happen anyway. Rewarding your dog for a job well done encourages them to do that behaviour again.

In summary, everything we have just spoken about may all seem a bit overwhelming, but once you get started you will quickly realise that it is more simple than you initially thought. Putting the effort in now, before your baby arrives, and getting a good grip on the essential commands will avoid a lot of stress down the road and prevent more serious behavioural problems. But just in case you are reading this book and you already have some serious behavioural problems, fear not, I've got your back and the next chapter is the one for you.

How To Raise The Perfect Family Dog

CHAPTER 4

....

Dealing with serious behavioural problems

In this chapter we are going to discuss more serious behavioural problems with your dog, such as resource guarding, possessive behaviours and reactivity behaviours that can often result in a dog bite. Many of these are common issues we see on a day-to-day basis at SDT. Ideally, you want to get a handle on these behaviours before the baby arrives, as it will make your lives so much easier, not least because some of these problems can actually be dangerous when you have a small baby or toddler (more on toddlers in Chapter 7).

RESOURCE GUARDING

Resource guarding is incredibly dangerous in general as it can nearly always result in a dog bite. So if you have a dog that resource guards you need to address this before the baby arrives.

Resource guarding is when your dog has an item or something of value to them that they are guarding and refusing to give up, which can often lead to them showing signs of aggression towards the person that is trying to remove it or come in between them and the item. Resource guarding can be directed towards people – sometimes all people or sometimes just certain people. For example, the dog may be fine with you taking something away from them, but not necessarily a child. Resource guarding can also be directed towards other animals.

The reason resource guarding is no joke is because 90 per cent of the time it is displayed inside the home and, as I have already said, it can result in a bite. The most common things that dogs are likely to guard are humans, sofas, beds, toys, food, bones and anything else they may have obtained that they shouldn't, such as a sock.

So how do we stop this? You implement what I call the prison phase. As harsh as this sounds, you must remember this isn't forever; it is just while you are working on curbing this behaviour. You also need to make sure that the dog has an understanding of the command 'Leave it', covered earlier in the book (see pp. 53–6), and that you are working on this as you go through the prison phase, with the dog on a lead during the training.

The prison phase system is where your dog always goes in its crate when it's unattended. This way it is not in a position where it can get things that it shouldn't and that it could potentially guard. The dog goes in the crate for a couple of hours at a time. When it comes out, it comes out on a lead, and you hold that lead. You work on your training with the dog, on your basic obedience and general training, and you incorporate 'Leave it' – but *not* via a tug-of-war game. You use 'Leave it' with the dog on the lead after a vigorous training session or play session and then you can chill out with your dog on the sofa (as long as it's not guarding that) or on the floor working on 'Down', and then it's back in the crate. Repeat this routine for a week. After a week of intense training, you can slowly introduce the items that have become problematic again, increase the time spent out of the crate on a lead, and start to allow more leeway. By this time, 'Leave it' should be more bombproof and the dog's listening will be stronger. You can try to introduce toys again, such as balls, but never leave the dog to its own devices with them.

If it's the sofa that the dog is guarding, you can start to invite them on it for short periods of time. Using a training lead, I would also have the dog get off the sofa every time a human goes to sit down and then wait to be invited back on. This means if the dog is on the sofa with you, and your partner walks towards the sofa, you or your partner gets the dog off the sofa, and then once you're both comfortably sitting you then invite the dog back on. This will also help if the dog guards you on the sofa from other family members. Another example is if the dog is on the sofa and you get up, perhaps to make a coffee; when you walk back into the room get the dog off the sofa before you sit down, and then invite the dog back on the sofa with you.

If the resource the dog is guarding is you, then separation is required. Don't let the dog follow you from room to room for a bit. Don't let the dog sit in front of you by your feet. Similarly, don't have the dog in front of you if people outside the house approach you. Instead, teach your dog the 'Away' game for people who approach you in the house. This game is simple: you say 'Away' and throw a treat, which gets the dog to move away to get it. Send it 'Away' and have the other person come towards you. This command can also come in handy in other areas. You can do this if you are at home and the dog has sat next to you when you didn't want it to.

You also need to make sure that you are not creating a needy dog, because dogs that resource guard their owners can often have separation anxiety from them as well. A lot of the same rules – such as not fussing the dog when it's being needy, not letting the dog follow you from room to room, and teaching the dog to spend short periods of time by itself – need to be applied to a dog that has separation anxiety.

REACTIVITY TO DOGS AND/OR PEOPLE

What is reactivity?

Reactivity is a blanket term and one that is quite often misunderstood. Reactivity can cover lots of behaviours, from whining, barking and lunging to a full-blown attack and bite on someone or something. Any excessive barking that you haven't asked for, be it at home, in the garden or out and about, is reactive and anxious behaviour, and is a sign your dog is stressed.

People assume that a reactive dog is an aggressive dog, but that's not always the case. Even 'friendly' dogs can be reactive. For instance, if your dog is barking while charging over to someone, even if it's not going to bite them this is still classed as reactive behaviour and can be dangerous. If your dog is small and might not seem to pose a threat to a much larger dog it approaches in this way, since other dogs don't care about size, it is still reactive behaviour and can still be dangerous for all those involved. Even barking at passers-by from your car is reactive behaviour.

In many cases reactivity can lead to full-blown aggression. I define an aggressive dog as one that will physically do harm to another dog, another animal or a person. If your dog is aggressive and a bite risk, make sure it is muzzled as a safety precaution and don't wait another minute to call in a trainer. Dogs that have bitten will likely bite again because they have learnt it achieves the result they want (usually that the thing/person the dog is reacting to moves away). Wearing a muzzle to avoid any further bites can be the difference between your dog remaining with you or being seized and put to sleep.

Prevention and cure

There are so many reasons why your dog might be reactive, but regardless of where the reactivity is coming from, I am going to go through some basics that can help any dog with such behaviour. These techniques can also be used with a dog that's not reactive as a way of preventing reactivity from happening. Much of the information deals with seeing another dog as a trigger, but the methods work just as well with anything that your dog reacts to, including cars and bikes. Along with what you've learnt so far from this book, learning these general approaches will be a game-changer.

The first thing you are going to focus on is lead reactivity. The reason for this is simple. Your dog should not be off the lead if it's reactive, especially if it's going to go charging over to someone or something. Often, when the lead reactivity part is fixed, the rest will follow.

It's also important to note that if you've mastered my three core principles from Chapter 3, if you have addressed the issues in the house, and if you are consistent in all other areas, major problems like reactivity are much easier to address and resolve themselves much quicker. You have to look at dealing with reactivity as you would building a house: you don't start with the roof as there would be no foundations to lay it on and it would just collapse. Well, reactivity is the roof, and to really fix it you must cement your foundations.

So, if you want to resolve reactivity, first you need to nail the lead walking, then you need to make sure you are relaxed, and you want to give the dog something to focus on.

Sniff your way to success

Reactive dogs are a bit like snipers: they are just using their eyes and looking around, waiting for a stimulus to explode at. More often than not, reactive dogs are visually oriented, and they very rarely use their nose. So, you want to get that nose engaged instead.

Remember, a dog takes in information through their nose; it's such a powerful thing and when they are using it, they are often curious and focused. For a dog, sniffing is mentally enriching and helps calm them down, so you need to encourage the use of the nose more to help with reactivity.

How do we do this exactly? The answer might surprise you . . . because you use the eyes! It's time to practise the art of attention. I like to use a clicker with reactive dogs. You need to make sure the dog understands the clicker first, but the clicker is how we will get that nose engaged. It's simple really – you use the clicker as soon as your dog sees a trigger (something it's likely to react to). But the real secret is to click the clicker *before* your dog has a chance to react. Your dog will hear the clicker and focus on you because, through your earlier training, your dog has already associated that clicker sound with the fact a treat is coming (most likely food!).

Next, you move backwards with a handful of treats, for a few steps, luring the dog towards you, thus creating some space between your dog and the trigger, and then you drop the treats on the floor. Now the reason you put the treats on the floor is because it keeps the eyes down, away from the trigger, engages the nose and drags out the reward. It becomes more rewarding and more enriching for the dog. But don't worry, this won't encourage your dog to search for food on the floor going forward; the dog knows the food comes from you.

So, it's: click before your dog sees the trigger, step back a few steps for space and put the treats down on the floor. Repeat this every time you see a trigger. What will start to happen is your dog will begin to look at a trigger and then look back at you for the expected reward. This also gives you an opportunity to click and reward. You are creating a pattern of behaviour: the dog looks at a trigger (another dog, for example), then looks at you and gets a reward.

This changes the dog's emotional response to how they perceive the trigger, so instead of it creating a stress response in your dog that leads to them reacting, it's now creating a feel-good response because the trigger now equals treat.

This technique is known as counter-conditioning. Here is some need-to-know information for this method:

1. If your dog doesn't break focus from the trigger when you click, stop clicking. In this situation, the fixation is too great, and you need to manually break the fixation instead. To do this, I like to pull up on the lead, turn into the dog and walk off, creating a bit more space. Then I start again.

2. Space is key in this method, so practising this in fields or other places where you will see dogs

– or where you can set up another trigger – but still have lots of room to work with will help massively. The more space, the easier it is for the dog to cope.

3. If your dog doesn't take food when it's outside the home, start to hand feed at home. This will help massively with your dog accepting food from your hand when out and about. Still drop the food as outlined above, even if the dog doesn't take it. Often the food will still bring the eyeline down and activate the nose.

The 'Sniff' command

I also like to teach reactive dogs the 'Sniff' command. It can then be used to prompt sniffing, which helps to calm the dog when you find yourself in a challenging situation. To teach this command, just say 'Sniff' and throw a treat on the grass or ground. Practise this action often and at random times when there is nothing going on for best results. If you see a trigger and your dog knows the 'Sniff' command, even if the treats are already on the floor and your dog is ignoring them you can use the command to get them to sniff and possibly take the food on the floor, breaking their focus and helping them to relax.

If your dog has a toy drive, you can also use toys to help your training, especially if your dog likes things like tug. Use the marker 'Yes' when your dog sees a trigger, step back and engage in a game of tug. While this won't engage the nose, it does engage in play, which can also help a dog relax.

And if your dog likes both, why not mix it up and use a combination of the above?

Top spots to practise

Some good places to take a dog-reactive dog so you can practise these techniques include somewhere like a pet-shop car park, or the car parks of woods and dog parks. Here you'll see plenty of dogs and people coming and going, but you'll also have plenty of space to play with. These methods also work in a proactive way, and going to places like these to work on your dog's behaviour will reduce the chances of it becoming reactive to other dogs too.

If you want to encourage more sniffing generally to help you with counter-conditioning, try woodland walks and country parks. A good 'sniff walk' (where the dog gets to use its nose for almost the entirety of the walk), is always a good idea. As long as your dog is dragging you along, a sniff walk is enriching, providing confidence and mental stimulation, plus it tires your dog out. This can help hugely with reactive dogs.

As you work with counter-conditioning, you might wonder how to measure your progress. A good indicator that you're successfully using the method is if you notice that when you approach a known trigger for your dog (e.g. another dog, a car, a person on a bike), instead of focusing on the trigger your dog looks to you, expecting a reward. When this happens, you know you're on the right track. When this happens consistently, you can begin to draw out the rewards, be slower to reward, and reward intermittently or randomly. You can also use praise rather than food rewards. Now you can focus on enjoying the process, happy that you've made progress. This emotion will rub off on your dog too, and less stressful walks will become the norm.

However, there's no defined timeline for working with reactivity. For some dogs a change in tools or mindset might bring an immediate improvement. But how quickly reactivity improves will depend on everything from how deep-rooted the problem is and how hard you work, to how consistent you are, your own confidence and the opportunities you have for exposure to triggers.

Reactivity to the doorbell

Reactivity to the doorbell is a very common issue that we get asked for help with. Now you might not necessarily mind your dog barking at the door right now, but when your baby has finally fallen asleep, giving you those 5 minutes of well-earned peace, suddenly the courier turns up and your dog begins to go mental. Having them react to the doorbell is not great in these situations.

Now barking at the door is completely normal for many dogs because they are naturally territorial animals and, in many cases, having them alert us to somebody at the door is not always a bad thing. But you want to be able to control this.

If the doorbell goes and your dog is reacting and you start shouting and jumping up trying to stop your dog, you are actually less likely to stop the dog barking as, through the dog's eyes, it actually looks like you are joining in with them.

So how do we stop this? You need to start practising before the big game. Get somebody, maybe another member of your household or a friend, to help you, or even download an app that plays doorbell sounds. Either way, you want the doorbell to go off with you in the house as normal. Let the dog go running to the door, casually get up, go over to your dog that is at the door and pick up the lead – because remember, if your dog is not trained it should be on an indoor lead. Pick up the lead, say 'Enough' in a stern voice, then lead the dog to its bed or crate, and if the dog is quiet, reward the dog. If your dog understands that 'Place' means 'Place', or they are in the crate, then they should know what to do, which is to wait to be released. You need to repeat this many times, at random moments throughout the day, so that the sound of the doorbell means 'go to your bed and good things happen'. What we are effectively doing here is changing the association to the sound of the doorbell. So instead of the doorbell meaning it's time to be on guard, or party time, let's go crazy, it will now mean something positive and your dog will understand what is expected of them.

Reactivity to visitors

Reactivity to visitors is a big, big problem, especially with a new baby, because many people are sure to want to come round to see you and the new addition to the family. Not having to worry about your dog will make the process so much more pleasant.

So how do we begin to help this? First things first, you need to have mastered the reactivity to the doorbell as this will help tremendously. You also need to make sure that if people are coming round and your dog is a bite risk, that it is muzzled. You also need to make sure that you are calm when people come round, because if you are worried about your dog, it will not understand that you are worried about them; it will just know that you are worried every time somebody comes round and your dog will misinterpret this as the person coming round being the one that has you worried.

So when somebody does knock on your door or ring your doorbell, your dog should go to its bed. You should then be able to open the door and instruct your guests to completely ignore your dog, not to stare at your dog, not to talk to your dog and act as if the dog doesn't exist. If your dog comes off its bed, remember to pop it straight back on it. When your dog is calm, you may release it from its bed. But I recommend if this is the first time the dog is meeting a person to keep space between that dog and the person, ensuring you reward your dog for any good choice it is making.

You can also have your guests just throw treats in the direction of your dog to sweeten the deal. Your guests should never directly give your dog a treat from their hand (see below).

Why does this work?

In the past, people were often told to hold out a treat for a nervous dog to come and take. But for a nervous and/or reactive dog, coming to you to take it from your hand sets off conflicting instincts. The first reason for this is that when a dog gets nervous it often isn't using its nose but its eyes. Holding out a hand for the dog to sniff or to offer a treat means the dog's eyes are just focused on what makes them uncomfortable and can be mistaken for you trying to touch them. That can trigger a reaction. Even a dog that has been brave enough to come and take the treat can quickly panic and retreat as it gets closer, and potentially react.

Instead, when you throw the treat you are giving the dog space, which is key for a reactive and nervous dog to feel comfortable. When you throw the treats over the dog's head, you've created a positive-only association as there's no need to approach the scary thing to get the reward. As the dog snuffles for the treat, the nose becomes engaged, and using its nose automatically relaxes a dog. Your guests should now go into the main room of the house and behave normally. Note that you still have hold of the dog's lead at this stage, and you can continue to throw treats to build up the dog's confidence.

On the guest's second visit, if your dog is nervous but not reactive, you can let the dog go over to the person to sniff but, again, *no touching, no talking, no staring and no holding hands out.* Here your aim is for the dog to be able to sniff on their terms, as using their nose is what will help the dog relax and gather information. Sniffing is a ritual that you must let the dog complete; when it's done, the dog will either walk away, which means they're not interested in the person, or the dog will sit and present themselves to your guest. If the dog does the latter, then your visitor can offer a treat with their hand low by their side, but I would avoid stroking for the first visit or two so the dog gets to know the person better.

If the dog has a history of lunging at guests, it's best not to let it go over to sniff newcomers on their first visit to avoid any upset. Just the presence of the person who is following the rules outlined above and creating a positive association will have a lasting impact. On the next visit, you should be able to move on to the sniffing stage. Once the dog has seen the person and you've followed all the above, you can either keep the dog on the lead next to you or send it to its crate to switch off, preferably with the crate in the room where you guys all are during these visits.

Getting a dog used to someone new coming into the home is a bit like dating. Have your guest play hard to get; don't give it to them all on the first date, leave the dog wanting more. Don't rush or force the relationship, just enjoy the process. The more times the dog sees that person, the easier it gets.

Good days and bad days

It is important to understand that when you are training a dog, or even when you have children, or just life in general, that you are going to have good days and bad days. That's completely normal and absolutely fine. When you are training your dog, particularly if your dog has some behaviour problems that have been going on for a while, it is normal to get frustrated or disheartened that it is not always going to plan. At the end of the day you are dealing with a living being, not a robot. Sometimes dogs are enthusiastic and want to work, but sometimes, like us, they can have an off day. It's all part of the learning process.

If you are training your dog and it's not going to plan, take a step back, do something easy that you know the dog knows well, even if it's just a basic sit or a basic down. Do this and then reward the dog. Spend some time doing something easy, because, as silly as it sounds, if the dog is getting many wins, they're going to feel better about themselves and it's going to impact your emotional wellbeing. Then continue later on or even the next day when you go back to what you were initially trying to do.

Sometimes we get lost, guys. Sometimes, particularly when you start seeing improvement, you can get carried away and start asking for too much, or push the dog too hard and you can forget why you are doing this in the first place. And in pushing too much and asking for too much, you can kill the dog's enthusiasm. So it's important you remember you are doing this because you want a happy dog and a happy life, and a better-behaved dog. Something I like to do with my dogs if I'm having a bad day is just go somewhere quiet, where there are next to no people around – the middle of the woods, or just a walk in the middle of nowhere – and forget about such formal training and just let the dogs be dogs, let them sniff, explore and just have fun. All while I just sit back and watch, and amongst the peace it helps me to relax, and then this makes me motivated to start again tomorrow.

As a new parent it can be hard – lack of sleep, the constant attention you need to give to your children, feeling like you have no time for yourself. It can make you feel run-down very quickly. On days like these, it is always best not to expect too much from your training, or even give yourself a day off, because your mood massively impacts the dog. The reality is you don't need to do hour-long training sessions multiple times a day. Hell, you don't even have to do 20-minute sessions multiple times a day. As the old saying goes, a little goes a long way. All those little blocks of 5 minutes here, 5 minutes there all add up and leave a lasting impact on your dog's behaviour. Remember that three-point formula I mentioned earlier (see pp. 28–34)? Just making sure that bit is covered will make your life easier and improve your dog's behaviour.

Finally, if you find yourself having more bad days than good days, it is okay to ask for help, whether that is help for you, for your child or for your dog. There is no shame in asking for support, so don't ever feel like you have failed by doing so. Being a mum is hard, being a dad is hard, being a dog owner is hard, but it is worth it in the end.

CHAPTER 5

. . . .

Bringing the baby home

So the big day is finally here. Congratulations! The moment you have been waiting for, the moment that is going to change your life. Hopefully it will go a lot smoother for you than it did it for me with the birth of my second child, Grace. Funny story: I got the call from my wife to say she was going into labour. At the time, I was about 40 minutes away from home (we were having a home birth), out walking a bunch of clients' dogs. I had to race to drop off each dog one by one back to their owners while in a state of sheer panic! Then, once all the dogs were safely back home, I made the 20-minute drive back home to my wife, making every traffic violation along the way (probably). As I was turning into my road, the house mere moments away, I got stuck behind a bin lorry, so I had to turn around and race around the block. As I pulled up, I got a phone call to say my beautiful baby girl had arrived. She was born on the living room floor; she had actually arrived quicker than the ambulance and we had an unexpected home birth. I did, however, still get to the cut cord. So hopefully your experience will be much smoother than mine!

Now before we get into bringing the baby home, let's talk about what you are going to do with the dog while you are giving birth. As with all new arrivals, things can be very unpredictable; you could be away for any anything from 20 minutes to 72 hours. As you've just read, my wife was closer to 20 minutes, while my business partner's wife was 72 hours! Bearing this in mind, it is a good idea to have someone on call that can take care of your dog at the drop of a hat around the time of your due date. A good family member, friend or a trusted neighbour is ideal. Failing this, pet-sitters or dog walkers can also be great in your time of need.

So now you need to bring that bundle of joy home and introduce them to the house and, of course, your dog. I always recommend, where possible, you have somebody go home ahead of time. For example, the father or another family member or friend could go home initially to walk the dog and pop it into the crate afterwards, then you can bring the baby home. This will help release any pent-up energy and help the dog to relax, making the first interaction easier for you.

When you enter your home, and before you let the dog out of its crate, get everything setup for yourself, whatever that may be. Whether that is sorting out the changing bags, dealing with the baby, or even if it is just to have a cup of tea and 5 minutes to yourself. Do this first.

When you are ready, you can invite the dog out of the crate with the dog on a lead. The lead is very important here. Do not let the dog come straight over and sniff the baby. When it is sniffing the baby, it is important that it is not in the baby's face; their nose does not need to be touching the baby to smell it. If the nose is touching the baby, they are too close. Control your space and send the dog away using the 'Away' command if necessary. The dog must be calm any time it is in your personal space when you have a baby with you. Always remember to reward the dog in the beginning for any behaviours you like, i.e. when the dog is calm around the baby. This initial introduction should be kept short and sweet.

Never ever – and I mean NEVER – leave the dog and the baby unsupervised, even for just a few seconds. It is not worth the risk. If you need to leave the room, either take the baby with you, or crate the dog. Even the friendliest dog on the planet can accidentally hurt a child – a slight whip of the tail, a paw to the face, even a lick to a baby's sensitive skin can cause harm.

Let's not forget about the dog

It is very important that, although your world has

just dramatically changed and you may feel very sleep deprived at this stage, you don't ignore the dog and forget about it. You still need to include and think about the dog in your day-to-day activities. Leaving the dog out and not giving it the attention it needs, just pushing it to one side and not having a clear routine for it, can lead to behavioural problems. It can even lead to some conflict between you, the baby and the dog.

You must remember that your dog's world has also now changed because there is a new human living in the home – a new human baby brother or sister for your dog. So as hard as it may be, no matter how tired you are, you need to make sure the dog is still getting its daily walks.

Make your dog's daily walk about them, and make it fun. The walks should be the way they used to be prior to the new baby arriving. However, I also want you to remember this: having a new baby is hard, you will be extremely tired and having a day to yourself is also very important. Missing the odd walk here and there is not the end of the world, just try not to make missing a walk a frequent thing.

When your baby is sleeping, they recommend that you sleep as well (to begin with). However, if you can and where possible, spend some time with the dog first, even just 10–15 minutes here and there. Give them a little bit of training, some affection, some grooming time or just chill on the sofa. All these things mean the world to your dog and they help keep them feeling included.

If, for some reason, you find yourself very stressed – maybe the baby has been up all night or maybe you are having an emotional day – then this is when interactive dog toys can come into play. I have been there many times myself, and in these situations interactive toys can be a lifesaver. What I mean is something like a Kong stuffed with their favourite food, or a snuffle mat, a brain puzzle game or even just hiding your dog's favourite treats around the house. These are all great ways of providing some mental enrichment for your dog to keep them occupied and to help tire them out. They also free up some time for you, so that you can deal with the baby or any stress you may be going through.

On a more personal note, I wanted to write about something very important to me: mental health, which is not talked about enough. I personally suffer from depression; I have good days and I have bad days. Some days, nothing negative has actually happened, but for no logical reason whatsoever I can just suddenly feel very sad and want to cry. I remember when I had my first child, it was a terrifying experience. I was responsible for this small, crying, pooping, innocent life. And that, ladies and gents, actually terrified me. When you top all that with screaming and sleepless nights, it can really take its toll on you.

What helped me, and what still helps me to this day, is talking to somebody. Whether that is a friend, a family member, your partner or somebody that is trained to help with mental-health issues. But talking is key. Shutting down or dealing with it alone will not make the problem go away.

As I have mentioned before, it is okay not to be okay all the time. It is okay to have bad days, but remember this: you are not alone.

CHAPTER 6

Growing together, from toddler to child

So now your hands are full, this is where the fun really begins. Your little one is growing up fast and this is the time when you are going to get countless precious moments that you will look back on for years to come. This is also the time where you need those eyes in the back of your head to be fully open! Because not only will you be keeping an eye on your dog, but your toddler will now move quicker than you think and want to get their hands on everything, including your beloved dog.

It is around this time that a lot of dog bites occur. But I don't want to worry you because, as I have mentioned before, for the most part dog bites are so easily avoided if you teach respect both ways. Of course, in the beginning it is going to be much more about you preventing the dog and your toddler from getting into sticky situations, but as your child grows and gets a better understanding of life and what is acceptable and what is not, it gets much easier. But for now, let's focus on the importance of teaching your dog and your child to be kind and respectful of each other.

TEACHING MUTUAL RESPECT

Respect is a two-way street when it comes to dogs and children. It's one of the most important elements that will help you establish and maintain a safe and harmonious relationship between child and man's best friend. Sometimes, however, when your child is in the infant stage, they may not fully understand that things such as grabbing the dog's tail or grabbing its ears can lead to a bite. It is your job as a parent, more so now than ever before, to have eyes in the back your head. You need to be ready to intervene at the first sign of potential stressful situations you may see. Before I go any further and go over some of the dos and don'ts, I need you to remember this golden rule – and you probably know what I am about to say as I've said it before, and I'll say it again:

NEVER EVER LEAVE YOUR CHILD UNSUPERVISED WITH YOUR DOG!

Now it's not just about teaching respect on the part of the child and educating them to be gentle and kind around the dog. You have to make sure that the dog's interactions are also respectful, gentle and safe towards your child. So let's get stuck in.

Your dog is not a climbing frame

This seems obvious, right? However, there has been a huge spate of viral videos circulating on social media every day, seemingly becoming more and more popular, which often depict a child climbing over a dog, and the dog showing visible signs of stress (I will touch upon body language in the next chapter). The parents often miss the signs that show the dog is stressed, which is incredibly concerning because most of these situations are dog bites waiting to happen.

It is important that if you see your toddler or small child trying to climb on the dog, you must intervene immediately and very calmly. While small children will not weigh a lot to us, they can to a dog. Their grip, their little baby knees and elbows can all be very uncomfortable, and we must understand that dogs can't just say, 'Hey, lady, can you get this small infant off me? I am very stressed and uncomfortable.' Instead, if they're uncomfortable enough they will often snap at the child as a way of correcting said child.

You must remember that even the most patient and tolerant dogs have their limits. Every time that limit is pushed, there is a strong possibility that window of tolerance is getting smaller. Their patience will wear thin and the chances of a dog bite increase. It is also not fair on the dog to be put in these situations.

Your dog will be much more tolerant of small children if it sees you being their advocate, which means stepping in to intervene – not getting your phone out and trying to film what you believe to be a cute moment, but one that is, in actual fact, a very dangerous one. By removing the child, the dog sees you as someone who is keeping them safe, and this goes a long, long way.

It works the other way around too. It is also important that we do not allow the dog to use the child as a climbing frame. They should not be climbing or jumping all over the child. A small child can easily get hurt, even if you have just a small dog; their claws can still be very sharp and can easily scratch young skin. Remember to intervene often, using indoor leads where necessary and falling back on your training to help you in these situations.

Grabbing, pulling, poking and prodding

Similar to using a dog as a climbing frame, the act of grabbing or pulling the dog around and poking or prodding it can often occur when the child is using the dog as a climbing frame, or even just when the dog is within reach of the child. Children can have a surprisingly strong grip, as you may already have discovered. When they are stroking the dog, they often have a tendency to close their grip on some fur and yank as hard as they can. This isn't the child's fault; it's just what they do! So when the child and dog are bonding and interacting, as I have already said multiple times, they MUST BE SUPERVISED, so things like this can be prevented. Things like floppy ears, wagging tails and slobbery jowls are all like moths to a flame for a child, so bear this in mind.

Stealing toys

While on the subject of grabbing, you need to make sure the child isn't grabbing the dog in uncomfortable ways, but also not grabbing things that the dog has. This is something I had to drum into my nine-year-old when I got Mila, my rescue dog. Mila is a very playful dog, she loves to have fun with the children and vice versa. We will cover child-appropriate play and activities in Chapter 8. But the point I am trying to make is that my daughter Grace had to understand when she could interact with Mila and when she couldn't. If Mila had a typical dog toy and came running over to Grace, play could happen. But if Mila picked up something and made a point of not going near Grace, instead going to lie down and chill out by herself, then this meant that Grace had to leave her alone.

It is also very important that the dog does not try to steal what the child has. As mentioned previously, you would have used some of the kids' toys to teach your 'Leave it' command, so this will come in handy here, should you need it.

Constantly having something taken away from you or having someone attempt to take it, whether it is the child to the dog or the dog to the child, can cause a lot of frustration and lead to problems.

Why hugging dogs is not a good idea

Contrary to popular belief, many dogs do not actually enjoy being hugged. Hugging in the traditional sense – i.e. wrapping your arms around the head and neck area of another person – can actually be seen as quite a threatening act to a dog. A lot of dogs will tolerate a hug, and some can even go on to enjoy a hug under the right circumstances. But we must remember, ladies and gentleman, this is not about what your dog will tolerate from you, the feeder, the trainer, the walker, the safety blanket; this is about small children. Your dog may not be nearly as tolerant and forgiving of them.

Many times when a child goes to hug a dog as if it were a human, you can actually see the dog pull away. It may even frantically lick the child. When a dog is pulling away and trying to lick the child, this is not affection, this is not a kiss. This is stress. The dog is actually trying to appease the child. If this continues going on unchecked, it could result in a bite – and one of the worst possible bites at that: a bite to the face.

Now I am not trying to scare you here – remember, we have a whole chapter coming up on safe things children can do with dogs, so everyone is a winner – but, for me, hugging is just not worth the risk when it comes to child and dog. After all, their face is right in the face of the dog.

Similar to hugging, children, particularly when they are young, have a tendency to put their face in the dog's face. We also discourage this as sometimes it can startle the dog and some dogs can find it stressful. Again, if the dog reacts, it is going to get the money-maker.

That is not to say that the dog can't snuggle up to the child on the sofa or on the floor. For me this is completely different to a hug, and providing you have taken the time to teach the dog how to behave on the sofa, then having the dog and child chilling on the sofa together in a natural, unforced way can actually make for a great Kodak moment. God help me if you don't get that reference!

Let sleeping dogs lie
This is the age-old saying that has been around since the dawn of time, and for good reason. This rule

should apply universally, not just to children, but also adults. So many dog bites occur when a dog is abruptly woken up from its sleep. Now we've all seen those cute moments of our dog perhaps twitching or making strange noises when it is sleeping. This means your dog is dreaming and is in a state of REM. During this time, if your dog is abruptly woken up, for a few seconds they can forget where they are and panic, and this could lead to disaster. If you have to wake a dog up, it is always best to do it before or after they are twitching and making noises. You should do it by calling your dog to you, as opposed to going over to your dog and physically waking them.

Speaking of going over to the dog, you need to instil into your children that when a dog is in its bed or crate, or maybe even over on the sofa asleep minding its own business, they should leave it alone. The crate/bed should be your dog's safe space. It should be a place the dog can retreat to and be left alone. I don't need to tell you as a new parent how constant broken sleep can become problematic, so please, for the love of dogs, let sleeping dogs lie. Teach your children from a young age this very simple important rule.

Dogs in kids' bedrooms

Sticking with the subject of sleeping, I feel it is important to reverse roles here a little bit, and make sure that the children are left alone where they are sleeping. This is, for the most part, easier said than done. If, for example, your baby is asleep in its car seat, don't let the dog go over to it for a sniff as the chances are the dog will end up nuzzling and waking the baby.

This also applies to your children's bedrooms. My dogs, Roxy and Mila, are allowed in every room of the house, barring the children's bedrooms. Call me old fashioned, but I do believe there should be some sacred rooms that are just off limits to the dogs. There is really no need for your dog to be in your children's bedroom – if the child is asleep, then why does the dog need to be in there? Not to mention that, unless you are actually watching your child sleep the entire time, your dog would obviously be left unsupervised in there, which, as you know ladies and gents, is breaking the golden rule!

Let the dog eat in peace

We have already mentioned that the dog should be in its crate or bed when your baby is eating. This should hold true for the entirety of the dog's life. If you are outside in the garden having a BBQ or down the pub enjoying the beer garden, then I would recommend taking a place mat with you so that you can use the mat as the dog's 'place' while you are eating. A dog should not be in your or your child's personal space while you are eating.

It is absolutely paramount to drum into small children that they are to leave dogs alone when they are eating. When a dog is eating, this is not the time for a child to go over to them, to stroke them, try to play with them or interact with them in any way. Food is a major resource for dogs, and as a result they can see it as extremely valuable. If you keep messing with them when they are eating, this is a quick-fire way for food aggression to start. The same rules should be applied if your dog is eating a chew or bone.

The situations highlighted through this chapter are common times where dog bites occur if mutual respect is not taught.

As I mentioned at the start of this book, on average three children a day are admitted to hospital through injuries caused by dogs. It goes without saying this is a very worrying statistic, and in nearly all cases they were totally avoidable. Most dog bites occur with children that are under the age of five, and these avoidable dog bites usually happen due to infants being unsupervised, or parents not understanding the dog's body language.

LET'S RECAP

◆ Do not let your child use your dog as a climbing frame

◆ Do not let your child grab, pull, poke or prod your dog

◆ Although some dogs tolerate hugs, and can even be taught to enjoy them, we recommend not allowing children to hug dogs

◆ Discourage your child going face-to-face with your dog

◆ When your dog is asleep, leave them alone. The same applies for when your child is asleep; the child should not be disturbed by the dog

◆ When your dog is eating, make sure your child leaves it alone

◆ When your dog has a bone or a chew, teach your child to leave it alone

CHAPTER 7

·····················

Understanding body language

It is very important to be able to read your dog's body language and understand what your dog is saying to you. Whether it is through their body posture, facial expressions or the noises they make, they will use different signs to let you know what they need. By paying attention to these signals, you can avoid potentially difficult situations.

When disaster strikes and a dog bite occurs, it is nearly always followed up by the owner saying, 'He's never done that before' or 'That came out of nowhere', but that simply isn't true; there is always a build-up before a reaction. We call this build-up the 'loading phase'. Imagine downloading a file onto your computer. The progress bar starts at 0% and goes all the way up to 100%. In this case, 100% would equal a dog bite. But most people miss the build-up to that bite. So let's talk about some of the loading signs you need to look out for, because by spotting these, you can decrease the chances of that bar getting to 100%.

LOADING SIGNS

These are the tell-tale signs that your dog is getting stressed.

1. A stiff and tense posture

If you look at your dog when it is lying down, relaxing or even just walking around, you can observe its body language and you will see that it is moving freely, its body posture is relaxed and it seems very calm. When something starts to stress a dog – maybe they have seen another dog or something they are likely to react to – you might see the dog become very stiff and tense. This is no longer a relaxed dog. You may also see your dog's body posture start to lower and look more arrow-shaped, like they are about to charge. Or the dog's posture may change to make itself look bigger, it may hold its head really high along with its shoulders.

If your dog is lying down and something comes into their personal space, you may see that these loading signs are accompanied by them turning their head away or holding their head back further than they normally would. You may even see what we call 'whale eye', which is where you can see a lot of white in the dog's eyes. The position of their tail may change (see p. 116). This can often be accompanied by point number two, a change in breathing.

2. Breathing speed

Often, when a dog begins to get stressed, the way they breathe will also change. For some dogs, their breathing may speed up to the point it becomes erratic; for others, their breathing may slow right down. Again, if you observe your dog when they are relaxed and nothing is going on, and pay particular attention to your dog's breathing, you can start to see subtle changes based on what is going on at that moment in time. Now let's talk about panting.

3. Panting

Panting is technically just your dog breathing. Obviously, with erratic breathing you may see heavy panting, but panting is one of those things where there can be a lot of misconception. You might have read somewhere that panting is a sign of stress, and this is true. However, panting doesn't always equal stress. For example, if you have been throwing a ball around for your dog for 15–20 minutes, it is safe to say your dog might very well be panting. If it is warm, your dog may very well be panting. If your dog is sick, unwell or in pain, they could be panting. And, let's not forget, certain breeds such as Mastiffs are generally always panting versus, say, a Jack Russell that doesn't pant anywhere near as much. So it is important to understand that context is everything when it comes to panting. The simple fact that your dog is panting is not enough of a sign on its own to signify they are stressed. You need to make sure you recognise the other signs too.

4. Mouth position, lip-licking and yawning

Fun fact for you guys: before a dog bites, its mouth is often shut. It could be for just a split second, from when your dog goes from panting, to shutting its mouth, to then striking. Before this happens though, you will often see a very tense dog.

Your dog's mouth being shut does not mean it is going to bite you. If your dog goes from a relaxed state where it is breathing normally or panting, but then suddenly becomes very tense, maybe it starts licking its lips, or has let out a couple of yawns and then shut its mouth, these can be very worrying signs. If, say, you had a toddler in the dog's space at this time, pulling at the dog or climbing on it, you will need to act fast as it is very obvious your dog is stressed.

So let's talk a little bit more about lip-licking. Just like panting, this is not a cut-and-dry sign of stress. If your dog has just eaten, you may see them licking their lips and this is completely normal. So lip-licking alone is not enough of a sign to always indicate your dog may be stressed, and the same applies for yawning. Yawning can occur when your dog is tired, but yawning will also often occur when you are teaching your dog something new for the first time and they are trying to figure out what you are asking of them. Again, yawning alone is not a guarantee that your dog is stressed. I've said it before and I'll say it again, context is very important. You have to look at the whole picture.

5. Ears and wrinkles

Again, I want to refer back to paying attention to your dog when nothing is going on, because this is often the best indicator of your dog's relaxed body language. Now obviously different breeds have different levels of wrinkles on their head and, of course, different size and shape ears. But if you take a typical floppy-eared dog like a Labrador, when it is relaxed, you should see very few wrinkles on its forehead and naturally loose, floppy ears. But as the dog starts to become more alert, or even stressed, you may see more prominent wrinkles and more erect ears. This is normally just a sign that your dog is more alert, but if it is accompanied by them fixating on, or staring at, something, along with some of the above-mentioned stress signals, then this could be a sign that your dog is getting ready to react. They might even start to become a little bit vocal at this stage.

6. Growling and barking

This is quite simply one of the most obvious ways your dog communicates. Dogs are naturally vocal in their communication and, despite what some people may think, growling and barking are not always bad things. When I used to play tug-of-war with Sammie, or if Sammie was playing with Daisy, my late Rottweiler, in a rough manner, then you would hear them growling like a pair of lions. But this was all play and nothing to worry about. Some dogs are naturally more vocal than others when they play. Of course, growling can also be a warning sign that your dog is uncomfortable. If your dog is in its bed or if they have a bone or toy, and your child goes over to them and your dog lets out a growl, this is a clear warning that your dog is not comfortable and could be on the verge of reacting.

7. Hackles (Piloerection)

This is an involuntary reflex response that often occurs during a state of high arousal. Often, when a dog is nervous you may see its hackles. This is the strip of fur standing up along the dog's back – it is a bit like the hairs on the back of our neck standing up when something doesn't quite feel right. If something was to happen and you see your dog's hackles standing up, combined with some of the other points we have spoken about with regard to body language, it could be safe to say that your dog is unsure of the situation. However, the hackles standing up does not always mean that your dog is unsure. When my late Rottweiler Daisy used to play with her boyfriend, Alfred the Rottweiler, they would run around and often Daisy's hackles could be seen standing up. I was never concerned by this, because the two of them were inseparable and in this case it was nothing more than just adrenaline.

8. The tail position

One of the biggest misconceptions in the dog world is that a wagging tail always means a dog is friendly. This is not true and many a  bite has occurred because people misinterpreted the meaning behind a wagging tail. When a dog's tail is wagging, this simply means adrenaline is going through their body. Just like raised hackles, this is a reflex response.

But what is important above all else is the position of the tail. If we take a dog swinging its tail from right to left with the tail positioned slightly up, almost in line with its back and their backside going ten to the dozen, this is often a dog that is happy with what is coming towards them. You will often see this most when you first enter the home. However, if that tail is held very low and wagging, almost in a tucked position, your dog is adrenalised but this could be an indicator that it is concerned. When you see this, don't stroke the dog at this moment. Because many times you will see the tail slow down, the dog start to tense up and this can sometimes be followed by a reaction. For more information on tail position, see the nifty illustrations below.

Tail motion explained

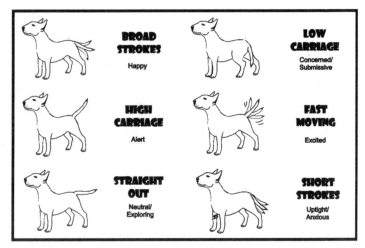

BROAD STROKES Happy	**LOW CARRIAGE** Concerned/ Submissive
HIGH CARRIAGE Alert	**FAST MOVING** Excited
STRAIGHT OUT Neutral/ Exploring	**SHORT STROKES** Uptight/ Anxious

Sometimes when a dog approaches you with its tail very low but wagging, they will keep their head and body very low as well. They may even roll on their back and expose their belly in a submissive manner. Again, you shouldn't stroke the dog here. Let's explore why.

9. Rolling onto the back and exposing the belly

This is often a submissive posture from the dog, but context is very important here. Often, if a dog runs over to your dog or vice versa, and your dog's body posture is very low, with its tail held low (even if it's wagging) and they immediately roll onto their back, they are doing this because they are actually very nervous and are showing that they are not a threat to the other dog. If the other dog stands over them, or if they do this to a person and the person touches them in the wrong way, they can quickly freak out and panic.

You need to make sure that if your dog behaves this way that you don't let them run over to other dogs. Or if a dog is running over to them, put your dog behind you and make sure the approaching dog doesn't get to your dog. Your dog needs to see that you have their back and this will build their confidence. If your dog does this when they first meet somebody, you need to instruct the guests not to interact with them until they are in a relaxed posture.

Now this is not to be mistaken for your dog wanting a belly rub – that is a very different story. Remember I said that context is important. If your dog comes barrelling over to you, tail wagging and with a happy-go-lucky body posture, and you start stroking your dog and they roll onto their back, chances are they just want a good old belly scratch, and that is absolutely fine! The key difference between your dog going into a nervous submissive posture and just rolling on its back for a belly stroke is the way in which they approach the situation. Something you might notice if your dog is in a nervous submissive posture on its back is that its tail will often be tucked almost onto its belly. Whereas typically when a dog is enjoying a belly rub, their tail is straight on the floor in line with their back, and you may even see it wagging.

In summary, guys, context is the most important factor. Somebody once asked me on Instagram if I ever get sick of repeating myself. And the long and short of it is, no I don't, and it is simply because when I am repeating myself, it is usually because it is extremely important information that people need to know about dogs. As I said, study your dog when nothing is going on. Without sounding creepy, watch them when they sleep! Watch them when they are just lying down resting. Watch them when they move from one place to the next. Watch them when they are running, because often your dog will be displaying their calm natural body postures during these times. And if you become an expert in this it becomes much easier to notice subtle changes in their body language.

CHAPTER 8

....

Getting children involved in training

In this chapter we are going to discuss some fun ways you can get the children safely involved with some training and day-to-day activities they can do with the dog. It is very important, and should go without saying, that all the activities we are going to discuss must be supervised for safety reasons. Now if you know what I'm like, which as you bought this book I assume you may, I tend to spend a lot of my time telling parents about the things they shouldn't do for safety reasons, but in this chapter, I am going to turn this around and cover the dos.

CHILD-FRIENDLY DOG ACTIVITIES

The following activities and training sessions are age-dependent; some will not apply to your toddler right now, but you can build towards them. So without further ado, let's get stuck in!

Feeding your dog

This is one of the easiest activities you can get your child involved in, as long as they are old enough to participate. Where possible, I always like my children to feed the dogs. Because I feed them raw food, I always prepare the food myself and put it in their bowl. But then I will pass the bowl over to my children and get them to ask the dogs to sit. We then wait for eye contact from the dogs and get the kids to put the bowls down and get them to say 'Break' to release the dogs from the sit. The word you use is up to you. I use 'Break' as it is a unique-sounding word, whereas 'Okay', for example, is used too often in day-to-day life. I like to keep my dog-training commands unique to avoid confusion. Once the dogs begin to eat their dinner, I then ensure my children thoroughly wash their hands.

If your dog is particularly excitable around food, then a quick and easy safety protocol should be implemented through the use of your indoor training lead. You, the parent, holds the lead to ensure the dog does not rush over to your child, potentially knocking them over, or attempting to steal the food.

Getting your child involved in the feeding is a great relationship-building exercise as food is a very primal thing for dogs. You can earn a lot of doggy brownie points by bringing them their food, but also by controlling the food and making sure there are rules surrounding when and how they get it. Bringing your child into this process is a great way of teaching mutual respect between dog and child.

Lead walking

While we are on the subject of relationship building, I want to talk about lead walking and how getting the children involved in this activity can be very beneficial. As mentioned earlier, lead walking done correctly is a very powerful thing between you and your dog.

So how we do we get the child involved safely? It is actually far easier than you may think. What you need to do is get your child their own special dog-walking lead. I recommend you allow the child to pick the lead; the only stipulation is it must be slightly longer than the lead that you use to walk the dog.

Now you attach the lead as you would normally, preferably to their collar, as you do when you're going on a walk. You then attach your child's lead, preferably to a harness. By doing this, you maintain control of the dog, but the child feels like they are walking the dog too. This activity is especially good because it kills two birds with one stone: you get to walk your dog and get their energy out, as well as the child's energy – and trust me they are full of energy at this age! This is a great family activity.

Fetch

Speaking of in-garden activities, but also activities you can do outside the house, fetch is one of the most fun games you can play with your dog. Fetch is pretty self-explanatory. You throw a toy – usually a ball – the dog chases it, and, in an ideal world, it will return it to you and drop it at your feet.

Getting your child involved in this fun activity is another great way of bonding. I recommend giving the child a ball launcher to use as it will be easier for them to pick up the ball (this saves them having to reach down to get the ball with their small hands).

Now for a couple of tips on safety while playing fetch. Your dog must understand 'Leave it', and show no resource guarding issues over toys. In the beginning, the dog should also be on a lead with you holding it so that you can make sure your dog is under control. You also want to instruct the child to ask the dog to do something, for example a sit or a down, before they throw the ball. I know this is a little bit of common sense, but do let go of the lead as the dog will take flight and you want to avoid falling face-first into the ground.

Sticks

So many people use sticks during a game of fetch, but they are actually quite dangerous objects for dogs. During my time as a dog trainer, I have seen and personally had to remove countless sticks from dogs' throats. When throwing a stick, it is quite easy and common for the stick to land impaled on the ground, while the dog is excited and running over they tend to run up mouth wide open, grabbing the stick as quickly as they can, increasing the chances of it becoming lodged in their throat.

Balls

Let's talk about balls. Tennis balls are one of the most common types of ball used as a dog toy, but there are two things to bear in mind. Firstly, the material they are made out of is actually really bad for your dog's teeth. While they enjoy a chow-down on the ball, the small green fibres act as sandpaper and, over time, they will file down your dog's canines. A good substitute to a tennis ball is the 'Chuck It Ball' (there is a link on our website). These come in various sizes and fit in ball launchers, but are made of a durable rubber material, which is much kinder to your dog's teeth.

Which brings me on to point number two: size does matter – especially when it comes to balls. You need to make sure that the size of the ball is safe for your dog, and there is no chance it is so small that they could swallow it.

The last thing I want to mention about fetch – whether it is you and your dog, or your child and dog playing it – is not to overdo fetch and make it an obsession. Fetch isn't a game you should play daily; a few times a week will suffice. Too much fetch can lead to creating an adrenaline junky dog, not to mention posing a risk of injury, especially in young dogs that are still growing and elderly dogs.

Clicker training

Using a clicker as a marker to help with your training can also be a great option, particularly if you've got some more serious behaviours you want to work on, such as reactivity. But before you use a clicker, your dog has to understand what the clicker means, so the very first thing you need to do is make the 'deal' on offer clear to your dog. It's very simple: to let your dog know the clicker is a good thing, just practise clicking and rewarding several times over (click, reward, click, reward). The aim is to get your dog's attention on you, so you want your dog to look at you as soon as it hears the click. Once this is happening, you're ready to go.

The clicker relies on you being able to give your dog a treat, so if your dog is not food motivated, you may need to stop feeding all food from the bowl, and instead use the daily food allowance as rewards instead of offering any extras. This should help bring out your dog's food drive.

Playing in the garden

Did you know that just one pile of dog poo can contain a million roundworm eggs? In humans this can lead to stomach upsets, throat infections, asthma and, in some cases, blindness. Over one hundred cases of partial blindness are seen in children every year due to *Toxocara canis* eggs in dog faeces. So this goes without saying: clean up your dog poo before allowing your children in the garden. You'd be amazed what sort of things kids will pick up.

Treat delivery

The last thing I want to talk about is treat delivery. As may be the case with your dog or other dogs you have encountered, some dogs can snatch when you give them a treat. If this is the case with your dog, it is best to teach your child that when giving a treat they imagine they are feeding a horse. What I mean by this is they should hold their palm flat, so the dog does not nip their fingers. You can also teach the child to drop the treat on the floor or throw the treat if they find this easier or prefer it.

These are just some of the games and exercises I have practised with my children, and encouraged them to do with my dogs to get all parties involved. Whatever you decide to do, please always have safety in mind, use leads where necessary, and always supervise your dog and child.

The more you can get your dog and child doing things together safely, the easier your life as a parent becomes.

Conclusion

So we've come to the end of the line, ladies and gents, the end of what is possibly the most important book I've written – a book that needs to be out there because there simply isn't enough information available for dog-owning parents-to-be.

I hope you have found this book useful and that it has prepared you for what's to come as you grow your family and how to get your dog ready for that.

Being a parent is the most rewarding job in the world – in my opinion second only to training dogs! I'm very fortunate that I get to do both, and now you guys are doing the same.

If you ever feel alone, if you ever feel like there is no hope, please feel free to reach out. As a parent, I've laughed, cried, worried, been stressed, overwhelmed, and despite all that I wouldn't change it for the world.

Having a dog that's well behaved is key to making life better all around. So many dogs end up in rescue, so many accidents happen involving dogs and children. I hope that this book helps just a little, to start to reduce that number. If this book helps even just one struggling parent, then the months of writing this book have been worth it.

I want to finish the way I began, guys: thank you from the bottom of my heart, for taking the time to entrust us in helping you with your dog.

All my love,
Adam

Adam Spivey

Stay in touch:

Let us know how your training goes:

Facebook https://www.facebook.com/southenddogtrainingandwalking/

Instagram @southenddogtraining

TikTok @ southenddogtraining1

Twitter @_sdtofficial

YouTube @southenddogtraining1

A note about social media

Social media is a part of our lives and will be a part of our children's lives too. It's not going anywhere and we have to live with it.

The problem with social media is many people use it for the wrong reasons. Many people (mainly adults) use it to spread hate, tag their friends to rally with them on things they disagree with and generally will say things to complete strangers on the internet that they wouldn't dream of saying to them in person. I've seen good businesses come under attack from adults, because they disagree or don't like what they are seeing, instead of just scrolling past.

The problem with this is we have fully grown adults acting like bullies in a school yard. When our kids get social media, often they will see what us as parents are doing on there. Children are impressionable and observe what we as their parents do much more closely than we realise, so what do you think they will get from seeing their parents being mean or rude on social media?

We need to set a better standard for our children and make sure we are educating them to be kind and respectful, use their pleases and thank-yous, and treat everyone how they would like to be treated themselves. We need to encourage our children not to take to social media and bully, be mean or harass anyone, even if their friends are doing it. We need to teach children the art of being kind. We can't do that if we are not setting the standard ourselves. We can't do that if we are wasting our lives arguing with complete strangers on the internet and if we are getting angry with things we don't like instead of just scrolling on.

Let's teach children that life is so much more than selfies, so much more than worrying about the opinions of strangers. Let's teach children if they don't like what they see to keep scrolling and to stay out of other people's business.

Let's teach children if they don't have anything nice to say, then don't say anything. And that starts with YOU!

Index